THE
PATIO GARDEN

month-by-month

THE
PATIO GARDEN

month-by-month

MICHAEL JEFFERSON-BROWN

David & Charles

A DAVID & CHARLES BOOK

Book design by Diana Knapp

Colour and black and white artwork by Eva Melhuish, Avis Murray, Maggie Raynor,
Michael Lye, Coral Mula and Maggie Redfern

Photographs: Neil Campbell-Sharp: pp6–7 The Garden House, Hampshire, pp20–21, pp96–97
Fortress Road, pp122–123 Hillbarn, pp134–135
Garden Picture Library: pp8–9 photographer John Glover, pp106–107 photographer
Steven Wooster
Harpur Garden Library: p2 designer Patrick Presto, p3 designer Gunilla Pickard,
pp34–35 designer Michael Balston, Little Malvern Court, pp46–47 designer Keith
Geller, pp58–59 designer Keeyla Meadows, pp72–73 designer Jean
Melville-Clark, pp84–85 designer Anne Alexander-Sinclair
S & O Matthews: pp114–115
Clive Nichols: pp10–11

First published in the UK in 1997
Reprinted 1998

A catalogue record for this book is available from the British Library.

ISBN 0 7153 0534 4 (hardback)
ISBN 0 7153 0818 1 (paperback)

Typeset by ABM Typographics Ltd, Hull
and printed in Italy by New Interlitho SpA
for David & Charles

CONTENTS

INTRODUCTION

Although not a new phenomenon, several forces have combined to make patio gardening of major importance now. New houses and gardens are getting ever smaller and so available space needs to be fully exploited. Ease of travel has led to gardeners being more open to inspiration from all over the world and although our weather sometimes fails to make the alfresco meal the reliable feast it is in sunnier climes, the idea remains attractive.

Another important factor in the rising popularity of the patio is the general increase in leisure time and this applies especially to those of more mature years. Earlier and longer retirement means more time to enjoy the garden, though less inclination to masochistic back-breaking double digging or making the garden a work-out zone; comfortable seating on an attractive patio and longer coffee breaks are more welcome.

Patio gardening has as much importance in country properties as town ones, in fact there is nowhere that a patio cannot significantly enrich our lifestyle and allow us to enjoy our gardens more. But, perhaps it is in the towns and cities, where conditions can be very cramped, and a garden is sometimes a very limited affair, that the case for a well designed patio is most easily made. Here outdoor space is vital; some greenery, some plants and flowers to refresh the soul and suggest peace and relaxation are all necessary in an age not overflowing with tranquillity. Wherever there is stress and bustle, a place to rest our bones and minds after work or a spell away from home is invaluable.

An informal collection of container-grown plants include variegated agave (bottom right) next to the golden grass, Hackonechloa macra *'Aurea' and the sculptural yucca. The ducks rest below hydrangea and euphorbia and various climbers including wisteria and clematis*

Usually the patio is sited by the house so that it belongs both to house and garden, a transitional space which, while probably harmonizing with the house, is a self-contained area and has a character all of its own. The scale of a patio can vary from a small patch with a few paving slabs to a major construction. Its size depends on the ambience of the plot and the way you aim to exploit it. There is no need to suffer an unattractive patio or to put up with one that is dreary or does little to stimulate. One of the aims of this book is to point you in the direction of some possibilities and to awaken your own creative thought processes which may suggest ideas that have not been fully examined here.

The original meaning of the word 'patio' was an inner court open to the skies, something developed by the Romans and the Arabs, especially in Spain. It was a place of cool and peace, probably with water features and some carefully pruned trees. Although this is not what we now envisage with the word, a sense of privacy and retreat are valuable factors to include in any patio design. And inspiration can be taken from these original designs – walls, pillars, tiles and pots can be used to evoke Spanish or Moorish courtyards. The possibilities are endless.

A patio has the ability to exert a major influence on the atmosphere of both the garden and the home. It is worth giving it considerable thought, and planning exactly what you want before you begin. As with other areas of our organized environment, the somewhat opposing principles of peace and excitement have to be married in patio designs. Bold rather than fussy lines are usually more effective in the construction and it is the plants that are best used to add a touch of excitement. Think of the patio as a stage and the plants as the players: they can be used to soften hard lines, to contribute to the feeling of tranquillity and to provide their own drama. Garden centres recognising the

importance of the patio, often have examples to see – they certainly feature a wealth of construction materials as well as plants and decorative features to tempt you.

A patio, especially one that adjoins a house, has its own sheltered micro-climate that favours a range of plants less likely to thrive in more open aspects. Being close to the house, plants on or around the patio are more easily nurtured and the variety that capture our interest can become wider and wider: morning glory and daturas can be triumphantly blooming alongside traditional lobelias and pelargoniums.

If the house dominates your plot, it can be made to look more part of its surroundings by a closer relationship with the garden and the patio can create an effective transitional link. With limited space, a lawn may be an extravagance that once we have decided against it, can be seen for the time- and space-consuming element it is in a small garden. A paved patio may be augmented by gravelled areas or areas of wooden decking. Water can add real magic to the whole, perhaps as a pool with its still surface mirroring the surrounds, or as a fountain or spring with its sound adding liveliness. Then, with the approach of dusk and darkness, there is always the possibility of creating a new atmosphere by introducing lighting.

At home, unlike in our working environment, we have a real chance to create a pleasing, practical and recreational enclave – a latter-day Eden – and as needs and wishes change, we can alter our domestic decoration inside and out. Experiment is acceptable and, while there are no unbreakable rules of design, there are certainly mistakes to avoid and some ideas that are more likely to be fruitful than others.

The purpose of this book is primarily to be a guide to making, maintaining and exploiting the patio area. The year is covered, month-by-month, the flavour of each month being described in an introduction to the chapter. Following this you will find a list of possible 'tasks' for the month. Then 'Plants of the month' highlights some of the most useful patio flowers and plants for the time of

year; those featured are augmented by lists of others you may care to try. Then each month is allocated one or more projects that describe in detail how a more challenging piece of work can be planned and completed. You are the client, the entrepreneur, the designer and probably the contractor and builder too; you decide what will be attempted and when. This book is intended to be flexible – a project suggested for one month may be as well tackled in many others or not at all. You are free to organize your gardening at your convenience.

The skills of gardener and interior decorator are combined in the patio gardener. The hard-won knowledge and expertise gained in the garden proper has plenty of value on the patio, but in one sense this form of gardening can be quite different. The micro-climate of the patio may make the growth of many plants much easier, the use of containers and of plants in places with limited root room or by walls that are inclined to make the soil dry mean that skills have to be adapted. The plants of the patio are under more sustained scrutiny than in garden borders; we need to choose even more carefully and to tend them sensibly to keep them at their peak. Thus there is a much greater sense of intimacy with patio plants than those of the 'estate' and this gives an increased appreciation of their interest and beauty.

I hope you will find this book stimulating and full of ideas, not dictates. Remember that we garden for enjoyment and the patio can add to the richness of this pleasure. And, now to practical politics – to your own patio.

A patio with a useful twelve-month raised bed but here en fête with containers and hanging baskets: a suburban approach to the hanging garden of Babylon!

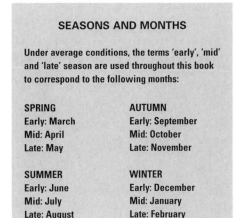

SEASONS AND MONTHS

Under average conditions, the terms 'early', 'mid' and 'late' season are used throughout this book to correspond to the following months:

SPRING	**AUTUMN**
Early: March	Early: September
Mid: April	Mid: October
Late: May	Late: November
SUMMER	**WINTER**
Early: June	Early: December
Mid: July	Mid: January
Late: August	Late: February

JANUARY

Even though it is just midwinter, it seems that the days are already beginning to lengthen again. Sometimes the weather is surprisingly good and it can be quite pleasant to venture out to do a little work in the open air.

The outdoor scene is swept clear of all the frivolities of other seasons; winter reigns supreme. The garden, and especially the patio, is stripped to its bare essentials, the underlying design lines and masses are unencumbered by excesses of foliage and flower, the initial plan has re-emerged. On patios built last year, stone and wood have mellowed and the bare branches of deciduous shrubs and climbers have defeated the newness that made them look just a little raw.

Weeding, watering and essential maintenance jobs of other seasons are not necessary or are reduced to a mere token expenditure of effort. This is the season to relish looking at the garden and planning changes, the time to consider the execution of the original grand designs, see any errors and look for any improvements that might suggest themselves – new ideas take root.

Not that the garden is wholly without the possibilities and probabilities of charm in this winter month. The patio and close by can be full of colour. Many winter-flowering heathers have been braving the worst of the weather for weeks; others are just opening their blossom. Snowdrops, crocuses and other small bulbs display their wares, as do many shrubs. Carefully planned hanging baskets and other containers are lively and bright with colour. This is going to be a great year.

tasks

FOR THE

month

**WALL PLANTS
TO PRUNE NOW**

Buddleia davidii
Clematis, jackmanii **group**
Honeysuckles (*Lonicera***)**
Jasminum floridum; J officinale
Roses, climbing and rambling

**WALL PLANTS TO
PRUNE AS SOON AS
FLOWERS FAIL**

Jasminum nudiflorum
Other somewhat later kinds
include:
Chaenomeles
Forsythia suspensa
Prunus triloba

CHECKLIST

- Pruning wall plants
- Planting pots of lilies
- Top-dressing
- Checking winter hanging baskets
- Seed sowing
- Checking frost precautions

PRUNING WALL PLANTS

It is wise to get many wall plants pruned before the end of winter if possible (see also p.136). Even winter-flowering jasmine may be ready for pruning by the month's conclusion some seasons. The idea is to cut back to two or three buds to encourage strong fresh growth to bear next season's bloom.

Climbing and rambling roses will behave better if main upward-thrusting branches can be brought down to angles closer to the horizontal. This appears to restrict the rush of sap and growth potential at the extreme end. It helps the formation of more flower buds and stimulates fresh new growth from lower down the plant so avoiding an extended trunk with flowering parts marooned somewhere up near the gutters!

PLANTING POTS OF LILIES

For a succession of bloom in pots, make new plantings of lily bulbs month by month. Use large pots and plant the bulbs low so that they can be covered with at least 10cm (4in) of compost. Use an ericaceous compost for Oriental lilies: other kinds will be happy with this or with a more general mix such as John Innes No 1 with half as much again of peat to help keep the mix open, moist, and slightly acid.

Procedure

- Use 20cm (8in) pots, or larger; not small ones.

- Cover drainage holes with perforated plastic or crocks.

- Using suitable compost, cover the base to 5cm (2in) depth.

- Place in three large or five small bulbs.

- Fill with compost to within 1cm ($\frac{1}{2}$in) of top.
- Label carefully.

- Water and keep cool.

TOP-DRESSING

This month try to find time to check any patio areas, paths

Winter jasmine: cut laterals to 2 or 3 buds when flowers are over

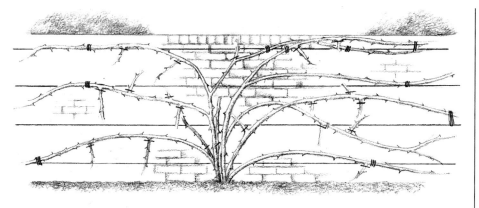

Climbing and rambling roses: cut back laterals and ends of main stems.
Bring pruned branches down towards horizontal and tie in

POTTING LILIES

All kinds of lilies can be potted now, especially good are all the Asiatic hybrids.
The following are dwarf kinds:

'Harmony', salmon-orange, Ht. 60–75cm (24–30in)
'Buff Pixie'
'Butter Pixie'
'Crimson Pixie'
'Dawn Pixie', pink and yellow
'Orange Pixie'
'Peach Pixie'

Pixie series bloom late spring–early summer and reach 35–45cm (14–18in) high.

SEED SOWING SUGGESTIONS

Snapdragons (*Antirrhinum*)
Bidens ferulifolia
Gazanias
Busy lizzie (*Impatiens*), in the light at 21°C (70°F)
Lobelia, bushy and trailing
Geranium (*Pelargonium*) – F1 and F2 hybrids and trailing kinds
Petunias
Verbenas
Zinnias

or beds that look as if they need freshening up with a top-dressing of gravel or shredded bark. A 10cm (4in) layer of bark will normally function well for at least three years. Worms bring soil to the surface of gravel, over the years destroying its neat appearance. A raking and a light dressing now will put all to rights.

CHECKING WINTER HANGING BASKETS

Severe weather – perhaps wind more than anything – will often have taken the gloss off the hanging baskets by now. Give them a lift by removing dead or broken pieces and, if necessary, introduce some fresh plants, such as winter-flowering pansies or foliage plants. If you have been well organized you may have held some of these useful standbys in reserve against just such an emergency, otherwise they are all readily available at garden centres.

SEED SOWING

Mid- to late winter is the busiest time for seed sowing. Choose the kinds you want to grow this year for bedding, for hanging baskets, specimens

and elsewhere. (See margin for suggestions.)

CHECKING FROST PRECAUTIONS

Plants in containers are subject to frost, not only from the top but through the sides as well. In hard frosts, bulbs can be thoroughly frozen and some may be killed, few plants will be undamaged by severe frosts lasting longer than 24 hours. Containerized bulbs and plants being brought-on to bloom later can be sunk up to their rims – or

even a little deeper – in various media such as peat, shredded bark, sharp sand, weathered ash or bracken waste. This will make frost damage through the sides far more difficult. On top some protection can be given by covering all with 6–10cm (2–4in) of shredded bark or a sheet of polythene-bubble insulation.

If you wrapped and tied semi-tender shrubs in sacking or other forms of sheeting, check that these are still secure and that there are not massive quantities of moisture around the plants.

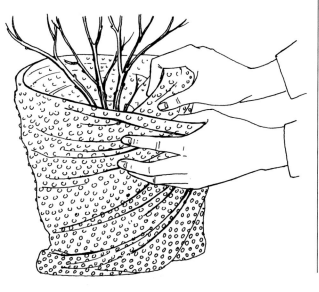

plants
OF THE
month

▼ SPOTTED LAUREL
(Aucuba japonica 'Variegata'*)*

A favourite of Victorian times and still widely planted, spotted laurel is one of the most long suffering of all shrubs and one able to perform well in poor soils and dark sites.

type	Evergreen shrub
flowers/fruit	Rather insignificant small bunches of purplish flowers. Females when pollinated by a male plant can produce tight clusters 5–8cm (2–3in) long of bright scarlet fruits, each 1–2cm ($^1/_2$–$^3/_4$in) long, persisting from autumn through winter
foliage	Polished and tough, pointed, oval leaves 7–20cm (3–8in) long by 5–8cm (2–3in) wide, bright green spattered with primrose spots. Persistent and attractive
height	2.5m (8ft)
spread	3m (10ft). Can be pruned to smaller size
soil	Indifferent to soil
site	Almost any. Invaluable for dark spots and poor soil where it is one of very few to manage well. Not swampy ground
care	Prunes well if needed
propagation	Layers or small cuttings which root easily
relatives	The type, *A. japonica*, is rich green; the popular cultivar *A. japonica* 'Crotonifolia' is heavily painted yellow, green taking a very secondary place; *A japonica* 'Gold Dust' is a dense bush with dark green leaves well speckled with gold

▲ BOX
(Buxus sempervirens)

A genus of tough, evergreen shrubs and small trees that will grow well in sun or shade, box will stand unscathed by the fiercest winter weather. Trimmed specimens can survive for centuries; the most important trim of the year is late spring.

type	Evergreen shrub
flowers	Insignificant, pale green and yellow; mid-spring
foliage	Oval, 1–2.5cm ($^1/_2$–1in) long; larger in robust forms. Dark green above, paler below
height	Usually clipped to restrict size but capable of forming a small tree 6m (20ft)
spread	Usually clipped but capable of 2–3m (6–9ft) sprawl
soil	Indifferent but should not be sodden
site	Useful in sun or shade
care	One of the premier shrubs for topiary, box can be clipped to many sensible, and some ludicrous, shapes
propagation	Layers or semi-ripe cuttings in summer
relatives	The most favoured is *B. sempervirens* 'Suffruticosa', a dwarf small-leaved kind, eminently suited to box-edging and topiary

WINTER JASMINE
(Jasminum nudiflorum)

A native of China, introduced into cultivation in 1844, this species proved exceptionally hardy and easy. Now it is one of the most popular of shrubs; but should not be spurned because of this; it is difficult to think of a garden or patio that would not be better for its presence.

type	Scrambling, deciduous shrub
flowers	Bright primrose on dark green stems; late autumn until midwinter
foliage	Dark green, narrow, pointed, oval
height	Climbing 5m (16ft) high with support of wall or tree trunk
spread	Wider than height. On the ground it roots as it grows
soil	Easy on all normal soils
site	Usually grown up wall, pergola, post or tree trunk but can be allowed to scramble down a bank or over a low wall – perhaps by the side of the patio
care	Wall specimens can be pruned back after flowering to encourage fresh new growth for next season's bloom. Support with wire or trellis
propagation	One of the easiest of shrubs from cuttings or from layers which it is always attempting itself
relatives	*J. officinale* is the common white-flowered, highly fragrant jasmine that starts blooming in early summer and can be still at it in mid-autumn. It has dark green pinnate pointed leaves and scrambling stems best given support up a wall, by a doorway or on to the pergola. Needs protection in cold areas

ALGERIAN IRIS
(Iris unguicularis)

Clump-forming iris with narrowly rhizomatous rootstock but so crowded and foreshortened that the plants look like leafy tussocks. Its robust performance when positioned close to a warm wall endears it to all gardeners. Flower buds can be picked and enjoyed inside.

type	Herbaceous perennial with persistent foliage
flowers	With long tubes acting as stems, rich lilac flowers, 5–8cm (2–3in) across, with yellow central flash; late autumn until late winter
foliage	Tough, narrow, evergreen leaves
height	20–30cm (8–12in)
spread	To 90cm (36in) with age
soil	Seems content on most soils except very wet ones
site	Warm sunny not too wet spot. Particularly good against sunny walls
care	Needs little care but dead foliage can be cut away
propagation	Divide clumps in early spring or early autumn
relatives	All variations of this fine winter flower are to be welcomed. There are white ones marketed as *I. unguicularis* 'Alba'; *I. unguicularis* 'Walter Butt' is a fine silver-lavender and *I. unguicularis* 'Mary Barnard' a dark violet contrast

practical project

DESIGNING YOUR PATIO

PATIO PLANNING

- Visit garden centres and gardens to see examples and materials
- Draw a scale plan on squared paper
- Mark out the actual areas with pegs and string
- Leave and reconsider shape and size

WHILE DOING THIS:
- Check likely sunshine around the year
- Calculate different levels required
- Work out material requirements and their cost
- Consider the timescale of the work – if necessary, can the construction be done in stages at different times?

When finished, the patio should be like an outdoor room, linked to the house and the garden. For a successful construction, that links the two environments well, choose materials that are sympathetic to those already present: brick for brick houses, granite for granite houses, and so on.

SIZE AND SITE

Size
There needs to be sufficient room to have chairs for sitting without crowding. Although this normally means that anything less than 3m (10ft) square is too small, you will know how many people you expect to use the patio at any one time and how much activity will take place there. With a large family and a barbecue you will need as generous a size as seems appropriate.

DESIGN IDEAS WITH STONE

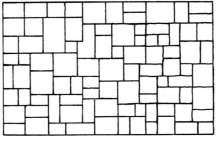

Random pattern with York stone

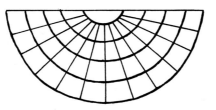

Semi-circular steps

IDEAS FOR WALKWAYS

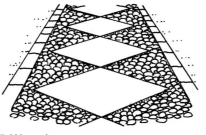

Cobbles and pavers

Site
The automatic choice is in the back garden, next to the house, ideally beside the kitchen door or living room French windows, but this may not be the best spot. Sunshine is essential to a patio; if possible we want sunshine day and evening, or at least for as long a period as possible during the hours when it is most likely to be used. This may mean constructing a pathway from the house to a more favoured position in the garden.

MATERIALS

As already stated the materials should reflect those already in the house and garden. The patio base needs to be solidly formed to take chairs and table safely. This still allows a choice of stone, brick, wood or concrete. If you have a brick house but prefer to use stone on the patio a sense of unity can still be achieved by finishing the edge with a strip of bricks or by surrounding the patio with a low-brick wall.

WOODEN DECKING

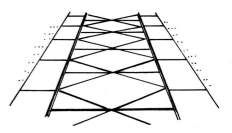

Bricks and stone

STYLE

Patios can be any shape or style; each site has its own ambience and there is no limit to the creative possibilities. Indeed, there is a danger of playing too safe, of doing what is obvious, hardly making a statement at all, yet there is also a need to balance the two warring design principles of excitement and harmony, surprise and peace. Consider your house. In it, there is the stimulation of treasured possessions and we may play with the decor to make it interesting and attractive; the house is a living space to be enjoyed, not a museum to be looked at. On the patio the same rules apply. The proportions need to be right, the different materials must marry together and the plants and people must gel. Use artifacts to give the design a pull in one direction or another; furniture and containers should both have a strong influence.

The feeling you can create could be strictly formal or almost cottagey. Close to a closed courtyard you could build a patio with a traditional Spanish or Moorish air. A pergola could dominate the whole, with growing plants around and above for an enclosed private area. You might like to make the patio like a balcony, with a cast-iron balustrade, or the deck of a ship, with a strip of water to compound the illusion. Take care with your design and create a sense of mystery.

(continued on p.18)

practical project

DESIGNING YOUR PATIO

(continued)

It is very important to decide whether you want the patio to give the feeling of being part of the platform on which the house is built – especially suitable with more formal houses – or very much a transitional space, a halfway construction betwixt house and garden. Visualize how it will appear from inside and outside. It may be close in appearance to a conservatory but without roof and walls, very much an outdoor room for alfresco dining. For the children, it may simply be a useful play area, one minute a space station, the next a toy racetrack.

A sloping site can lead to some interesting possibilities: two level designs for example. In this case it is sensible to make one clearly larger and the place where table and main chairs can be easily stationed.

Shapes

Frequently, a roughly rectangular ground plan is the most successful, echoing the house shape; a square form never seems as satisfactory as an oblong one. Or perhaps the configuration of the house and garden will make an L-shaped patio the ideal, helping to catch the sunshine over a longer period or enabling easier use of the barbecue. Adding steps or a path from the patio can make the entrance into the garden a more natural and pleasing matter. A low wall is handy for placing the newspaper open at the crossword and for the half full / half empty wine glass.

PLANTS

A patio without plants looks bare and unfinished so allow space for the positioning of containers, perhaps shrubs and maybe miniature gardens in troughs. If children are not a permanent feature of the household, some areas of the patio may be allowed to grow creeping plants in between paving.

INITIAL IDEAS FOR A PATIO

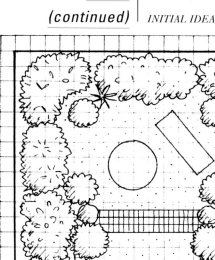

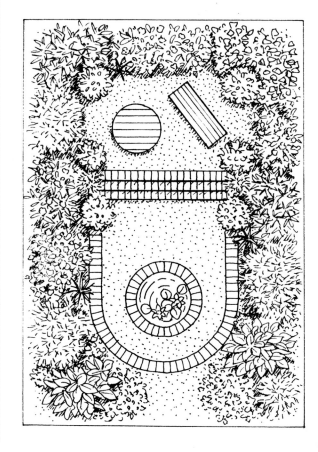

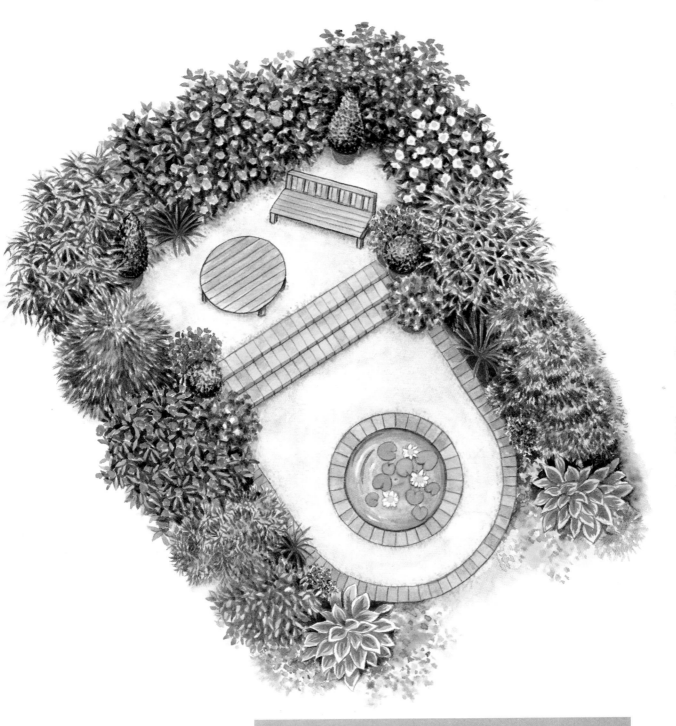

SEATING

When designing your patio, consider building seating into walls, especially if you are limited with space. A low brick wall can be made more sitable-on if given a movable slatted wooden seat and back (see also p.29).

FEBRUARY

Now there is no doubt about it, the days are lengthening and the bulbs are coming on cue to begin the big bonanza of spring. In full bloom, the early kinds are repaying the work of autumn, both in the garden and on the patio. Containers are bursting with the freshly-minted coinage of golden daffodils and silvery crocuses. Depending on last year's planning, there can be a lot of colour now or a more gentle introduction to bolder displays a little later.

This is perhaps the real beginning of the gardener's year, seed sowing starts in earnest and it is not too early to start the work that will ensure the patio is lively throughout the year – a stage with a non-stop revue of varied acts. Greenhouse, cold frames, conservatories and kitchen windowsills begin to fill with pots and trays of seed. Summer bulbs are being planted up in pots and containers. You might prefer to try to raise all your annual plants from seed or to save time and cost by investing, instead, in the small 'plug' plants appearing in garden centres. If time is a very precious commodity, wait till just a few weeks before the last of the frosts then purchase fresh, well-grown plants, almost at blooming size. You pays your money and takes your choice, or the other way about.

Now is the time to decide whether you want your patio to be full of brilliant carnival characters – petunias, impatiens and geraniums – most of the time or to depend more on foliage, and perhaps topiary, for a tranquil atmosphere with only the birds to interrupt your musing.

All is abundant promise, anticipation is a sizeable proportion of the pleasure of gardening. Towards the end of the month look out stored garden furniture and dust it down. Soon the patio will need its chairs and tables to look fully the part.

tasks
FOR THE
month

SOWING SEEDS

1 Fill the pot with seed compost

2 Firm and level the surface

3 Sprinkle the seeds on the compost

4 Cover with a layer of fine grit

5 Water well using a fine rose on the watering can and label the pot

BULBS
Bulbs planted in early autumn (see p.108) may be in flower now

CHECKLIST

- Tending flowering potted bulbs
- Planting containers
- Checking drainage and paths
- Trellis care

BUYING AND SOWING SEEDS

If not already done try to sow the more important kinds of seed before the end of the month.

TENDING FLOWERING POTTED BULBS

- Containers of bulbs that have stood out all winter are now showing signs of bloom. Although they need little

attention a top-dressing of peat, bark or gravel looks tidy.

- Daffodils, hyacinths and tulips that have been sheltered in a cool greenhouse, conservatory or frame will now be showing colour in their buds and can be moved into a suitable space on the patio. Groups of three decent-sized pots, half pots or pans look much more impressive than solitary ones.

- Some of the small bulbs such as the reticulata irises, snowdrops and crocuses are also coming into bloom now. These can be brought forward into the limelight from where

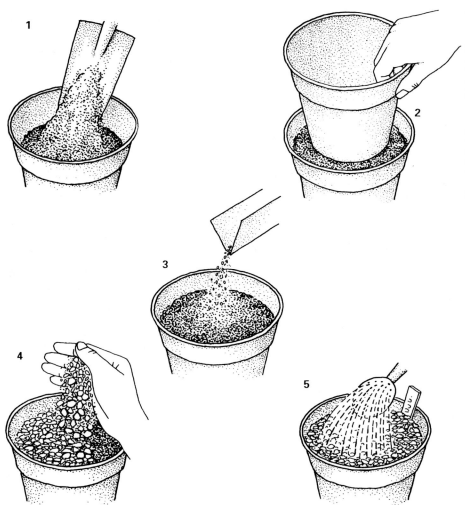

they have been waiting in the wings to make their longed-for entrance.

■ All these pots and containers are likely to be perfectly hardy and safe in the patio area, which is usually warmer and more sheltered than in the open garden, but even so if a particularly hard frost threatens they benefit from the protection of a sheet of polythene or even some newspaper.

PLANTING CONTAINERS

Containers can be planted at almost any time (see also p.40). Usually it is tackled in the autumn and late spring, but getting one or two done now will enable them to get established and will provide growing material over a wider time span.

Within reason, the larger the container, the greater its use and impact. Movable ones can be planted up with summer-flowering bulbs, such as lilies, galtonias and dwarf gladioli, together with plants such as scented-leaved geraniums (pelargoniums) and bedding plants. Keep in frames, cool greenhouses, conservatory or any frost-proof spot until the end of any danger from bad frosts, then bring them into their proper site.

Containers permanently on the patio can be planted with hardy bulbs to which geraniums and other bedding plants can be added later.

Alternatively, one or more larger containers may hold permanent shrubs or trees. Plant these now. The choice is wide but, bearing in mind that the ideal is year-round colour and form, evergreens will play a more telling role. Conifers are very suitable; the choice of colours and shapes is huge. It is best to choose the more groomed shapes and the brighter golds and greens

GROUPING LARGER SHRUBS

for real effect. If two or more containers are going to be used you can have matched or contrasting types (see margin for suggestions).

There are also other good evergreens, evergolds and eversilvers! *Euonymus fortunei* forms can be allowed to make their own informal growth or can be encouraged to follow more definite tailored shapes. Depending on how formal these are you might like to consider topiary, and box (*Buxus*) — see the project on page 132.

CHECKING DRAINAGE AND PATHS

There can be plenty of rain during this month and, with the ground already full of water from winter, this can bring some trouble with drainage. This applies not only to plants in containers but also to garden beds and to the infrastructure of the patio and the garden itself.

Patio surfaces should be

dry or only wet with recent rain. If they are constantly moist, this will encourage the growth of mosses and algae which can make the whole look unsightly and can make the surface slippery and dangerous. If the surface is constantly wet, provide extra drainage (see this month's project and the one on p.56). Avoid sodium chlorate, which when used as a weedkiller will encourage moss. Algae can be removed using a strong yard brush and an industrial detergent, usually available in hardware shops, markets or garden centres.

Pathways should be safe, weather-proof, dry and attractive. Brick paths can look very effective.

TRELLIS CARE

Treat trellis with wood preservative to lengthen its life. Check the trellis supports and replace any that have worn or worked loose.

plants

OF THE

month

SNOWDROPS

(*Galanthus nivalis* 'Flore Pleno')

This pretty relative of the daffodil is available in many forms. *G. nivalis* 'Flore Pleno' has much doubled flowers with the inner segments like many petticoats, forcing the three outer petals to a wider angle than in the more orthodox single form.

type	Bulb
flowers	Very double, white, with inner segments touched green; mid- to late winter
foliage	Grey-green, like miniaturized daffodil leaves
height	At flowering, 10–15cm (4–6in)
soil	All types, but best in open humus-rich soils where bulbs increase very quickly
site	Borders, between shrubs, hedgerows or in grass
care	Plant newly purchased bulbs 'in the green' just after flowering. Alternatively, plant dry bulbs as early as possible in autumn
propagation	Once established, lift clumps just before leaves die down (late spring), split and replant immediately
relatives	Many good ones: *G*. 'Atkinsii' is outstanding and tall with long, large graceful flowers; *G*. 'Magnet' has large fat flowers hung out like lanterns; *G. nivalis* 'Viridapicis' has green tips on all the six segments; and, of course, the standard, single *G. nivalis*

IRIS

(*Iris* 'Joyce')

This lovely, deep blue hybrid was bred from *Iris reticulata* and *I. histrioides* and perhaps outdoes both as a garden plant. These small bulbous irises can be very hardy and prolific outside if given exceptionally fast drainage.

type	Bulb
flowers	Deep blue with a golden central flash, 5–6cm (2–2^1/$_2$in) across; late winter or early spring
foliage	Grey-green erect, four-sided like straight skewers, lower than flowers but grow to 30–40cm (12–16in) after blooming
height	6–10cm (2^1/$_2$–4in) at flowering
soil	Best gritty open textured soil that drains well, acid or alkaline but not very acid

site	Sunny spot in rock bed, raised bed, pots or edge of border
care	Plant 7–10cm (3–4in) deep in early autumn
propagation	Lift and divide bulbs
relatives	*I*. 'Harmony' is very similar, *I*. 'George' is a rich plum-purple, *I*. 'Katharine Hodgkin' is larger, dwarfer and an unusual mix of smoky pale blues and olive-yellows

◀ EVERGREEN CLEMATIS

(*Clematis armandii*)

Unusual among the clematis genus as a fully evergreen species, *C. armandii* was introduced from China in 1903, the same year that *C. montana rubens* (see p.44) found its way into cultivation. Being so early and frost-hardy a place should be found for it, perhaps up the pergola or a corner of the house walls.

type	Evergreen climber
flowers	Usually in threes, cream, ageing pinky, scented, 4–6cm (1^1/$_2$–2^1/$_2$in) across; late winter to early spring and frost hardy
foliage	Dark green, polished, each leaf divided into three rather narrow oval leaflets and marked with three veins
height	3–5m (10–15ft) or more
soil	Well-drained
site	Warm, sunny
care	Easy in a sheltered spot, perhaps on a wall
propagation	Layer a low stem or air layer
relatives	*C. armandii* 'Appleblossom', a free-blooming clone with good-sized flowers

WINTER SWEET ▲

(*Chimonanthus praecox*)

Winter sweet produces its yellowish flowers on leafless stems from early winter to early spring. Although eventually quite large, this shrub is a relatively slow grower and can be kept smaller if necessary. The flowers have an enticing scent and are suitable for flower arrangements.

type	Deciduous shrub
flowers	Perfumed limy-yellow translucent outer petals and small maroon central ones, up to 2.5cm (1in) across; early winter to early spring
foliage	Dark green, oval, rough but shiny

height 2.5m (8ft)
spread 3m (10ft)
soil Rich and healthy, with an open structure and plentiful humus
site Very much best with the warm shelter of a wall, perhaps by a window so that the scent can waft in
care In an open situation only prune to take out weak growth; against a wall prune more extensively when established – as soon as flowers finish to allow plenty of time for the fresh growth that will bear next season's blossom
propagation Air layer
relatives *C. praecox* 'Grandiflorus' has larger, more yellow flowers; the rare *C. praecox* 'Luteus' has brighter yellow flowers

SCILLA
(*Scilla mischtschenkoana*)

Despite its name, a delightful low growing bulb that produces pale blue blossom from the time the leaves begin to poke through the soil. It is easily the earliest of hardy scillas and rates as the most useful species for the garden, being ideal for containers, rock beds or at the edge of beds or borders.

type Bulb
flowers Pointed bowl-shaped flowers, pale blue later showing darker blue central lines; several to a stem; late winter to early spring

foliage Low arching, shiny bright green, strap-shaped, relatively broad
height 5–10cm (2–4in)
spread 10cm (4in)
soil Any but not sodden
site In pots, miniature gardens, in raised beds, with heathers, or in the front of border
care Plant with 7–10cm (2–4in) soil over top of bulb
propagation Lift and split when crowded
relatives *Scilla sibirica* is much darker blue but of similar stature and form; early to mid-spring

SPRING ANEMONE ▶
(*Anemone blanda*)

There are many early spring anemones but few as easy and totally reliable as this one. It makes a lovely early touch of colour for a rock garden, woodland bed or edge of a border. It looks good close to the patio as it is without faults, lovely in bloom and foliage but quick to disappear when the spring party is over.

type Rhizome, sold as a knobbly 'bulb'
flowers Many-petalled, open blooms, often rich blue but there are splendid pinks and whites. Early winter, particularly in mild areas, but lasting through to spring
foliage Much divided, bright green, ferny leaves disappear a few weeks after blooming ends
height 10–15cm (4–6in)
spread 15–20cm (6–8in), more with age
soil Any that is well-drained, likes a gritty mix
site Open sunny spot in rock garden, between heathers, front of beds or in trough garden
care Plant late summer or early autumn, with 7–10cm (3–4in) soil over rhizomes. Leave undisturbed
propagation By sowing fresh seed or splitting rhizomes in late spring
relatives Named forms include *A. blanda* 'Ingramii', deep blue; *A. blanda* 'Radar', pink; and *A. blanda* 'White Splendour', a particularly large-flowered snow-white one. *A. apennina* is similar in foliage and bloom but has long, narrow rhizomes. *A. nemorosa*, the English windflower or wood anemone, has thin rhizomes and white flowers, blushing pink, but with some unusual pale blue forms

practical
project
1

CONSTRUCTING
YOUR PATIO

WARNING

■ *With any building job close to the house always be careful that you are not leaving soil levels above the damp course* ■

INTEGRATION
The materials used for pathways into the garden give a chance to link the patio to the whole by the use of similar materials. The patio edge can lead straight onto the lawn, with perhaps part of it marked by a low wall or a raised bed, or an area of gravel with boulders can be used to separate patio and lawn or border.

Mark out the contemplated patio area either with pegs and string, very clearly seen, or with hosepipe, sand or loose bricks. If you are going to have a pergola or trellis work as well, mark these with canes, or something similar, to help to give some idea of proportions. Leave this rough layout in place for a few days to ensure you are happy with your design.

PATIO FLOOR

The first step is to make sure the surface to be laid is secure, level and dry. This is vital, whether wood platforms, brickwork or stone slabs are to be used.

Foundations

■ Remove the top few centimetres – about 10cms (4in) – of soil. Turves or topsoil from the patio area can be saved for use later for potting or building up beds.

■ Build with a slight tilt away from the house to help shed rainwater.

■ If the site is badly drained take the opportunity to dig out a channel from the patio area to a lower spot or to a drain. Fill the channel with rough hardcore and cover with turf or polythene to act as a drain.

■ Use hardcore and washed sand or grit-dust to make a 10cm (4in) layer over the site of the patio. Ram the hardcore so that it is firm.

Paving

The middle layer between foundation and surface depends on what the surface will be. The easiest to lay and maintain is stone pavings. Ordinary flat pavement stones used for public areas are safe and uniform but rather boring. Much more pleasing is genuine York stone; almost as pleasing but hugely cheaper and easier to lay are the very good quality imitation York stones available at garden centres. The uniform depth of these makes it easy to construct an even surface. They come in a variety of sizes that can be fitted together to form varying patterns and produce a very effective random appearance.

LAYING PAVING

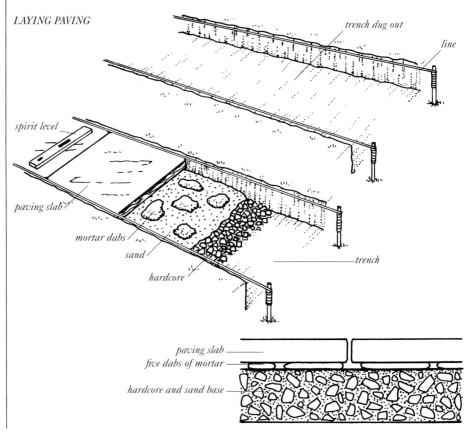

BRICKS

Bricks, old or new, matching the house walls and laid in a pleasing pattern, will add colour to the scheme. Old bricks could look well with a cottage-type dwelling. Being smaller and more inclined to move than paving stones, they are better laid in cement – at least in part, perhaps leaving one or two small areas where small creeping plants like thymes are allowed to grow.

Tiles

Patios in restricted sites, perhaps in heavily built-up areas or those surrounded by walls, could be the place to experiment with tiles for both floors and walls – at least in part. This imitates the design of Portuguese, Spanish and other Mediterranean patios.

Tiles might help to make the closed-in area attractive at all times, to suggest light and colour in the most dismal weather and they will certainly help to reflect any light there is. Any patterning is best kept simple and bold, leaving the plants the leading decorative role.

Gravel

Gravel has several advantages: it is cheap, easily maintained, clean and colourful; it also makes a good contrast of texture to other materials and, above all, it is plant-friendly. Gravel acts as a mulch for plants, keeping their roots cool and moist; it also sets them off well. Additional planting is easy without major engineering. Note: A possible disadvantage is that pebbles are attractive to small children and if very close to the house they can occasionally be carried inside.

MATERIALS FOR HAND OR MACHINE MIXING

MIX FOR FOUNDATIONS, 8CM (3IN) OR MORE DEEP

- 2 cement
- 5 builder's sand
- 8 coarse aggregate, 5–20mm ($\frac{1}{4}$–$\frac{3}{4}$in)

STRONGER MIX FOR FOUNDATIONS OF THINNER LAYERS

- 1 cement
- 2 builder's sand
- 3 coarse aggregate

MIX FOR BRICKWORK, WALLS, AND SO ON

- 1 cement
- 4 builder's sand

MIX FOR BEDDING SLABS

- 1 cement
- 5 washed sand

MIXING CEMENT BY HAND

- Work on a flat, easily cleaned, dry surface
- Measure quantities using a bucket, starting with builders sand
- Thoroughly mix dry ingredients
- Using only clean tap water, add just sufficient, in stages, to result in a mix that can be worked easily but is not sloppy
- Only make the amount required for the task in hand to avoid the mix drying before you use it all

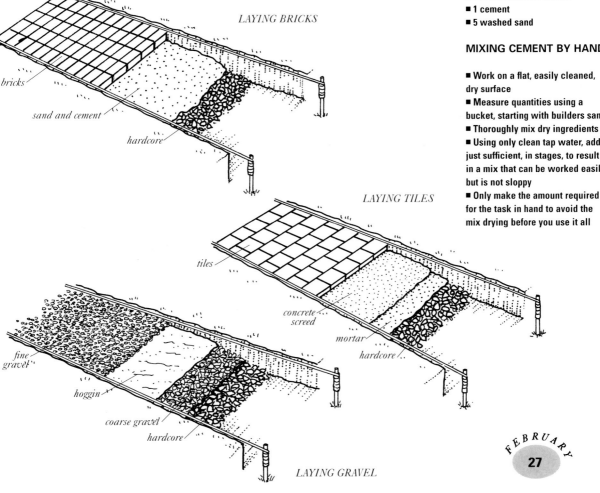

LAYING BRICKS

bricks

sand and cement

hardcore

LAYING TILES

tiles

concrete screed

mortar

hardcore

fine gravel

hoggin

coarse gravel

hardcore

LAYING GRAVEL

practical project 1

CONSTRUCTING
YOUR PATIO
(continued)

DECKING

Timber decking produces a further design possibility. Modern houses will allow the use of newly machined and stained wood while older properties may be better served with recycled wood with some patina of age. Colours range from a natural bleached near white or grey to the different stains offered at DIY outlets. The pattern in which the wood planking is laid can vary from longitudinal or lateral straight lines to herring bone or other decorative arrangements. The wood itself is decorative, its feel, its colour, and its textured graining adding to a soft overall effect. Square or oblong decking preforms are offered for sale; these are usually in one or two designs and in modules around 30cm (12in) square.

On flat sites, the decking may simply rest on supports just clear of the ground, however, where the ground falls away it can be taken out from the house as a platform well above the surface. If the height above the ground at the edge of the decking is more than 30–45cm (12–18in) it is sensible to design it like a wide balcony, complete with a safety rail. Obviously the supports for such decking must be completely secure, with uprights locked into the spiked metal post-holders used for fence or pergola supports, or similar. These holders prevent the wood being in contact with the soil and avoid premature rotting. The appearance is substantially improved by covering the ground below the decking with a few centimetres of pebbles up to 2–5cm (1–2in) in diameter.

■ Adjacent to the house, fasten the first horizontal bearer to the house wall with substantial masonry bolts.

■ To support the other bearers construct sturdy uprights. First, make generous concrete bases – not less than 22cm (9in) cubes – attach metal supports to them and then bolt uprights into these.

■ Uprights need to be at least 10cmsq (4insq) if distanced some 60–90cm (24–36in) apart, and substantially thicker if the distance is up to 1.2m (4ft) apart. They need to be at least 7.5 x 10cm (3 x 4in) standing tall, but could be 10 x 15cm (4 x 6in).

■ Secure joists to the bearer along the house wall and to the other bearers.

■ Link bearers together with cross-beams before attaching the decking.

Use wood planks around 2.5 x 7.5cm (1 x 3in) with somewhat bevelled edges for the top surface. These can be laid touching or preferably with a 5mm (¼in) gap to allow rainwater through. Such decking will need an annual scrubbing to forestall or remove any fungal growth. Strong detergent is sold for the purpose. Afterwards a top-up treatment of colour preservative may be called for.

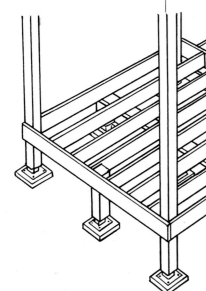
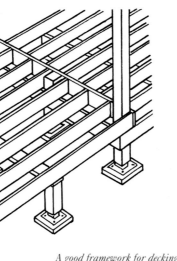
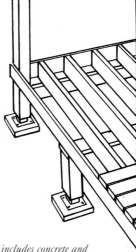
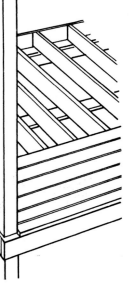

A good framework for decking includes concrete and metal supports for uprights. Planks (right) should be spaced to allow rain to run between them

STEPS AND **S**EATS

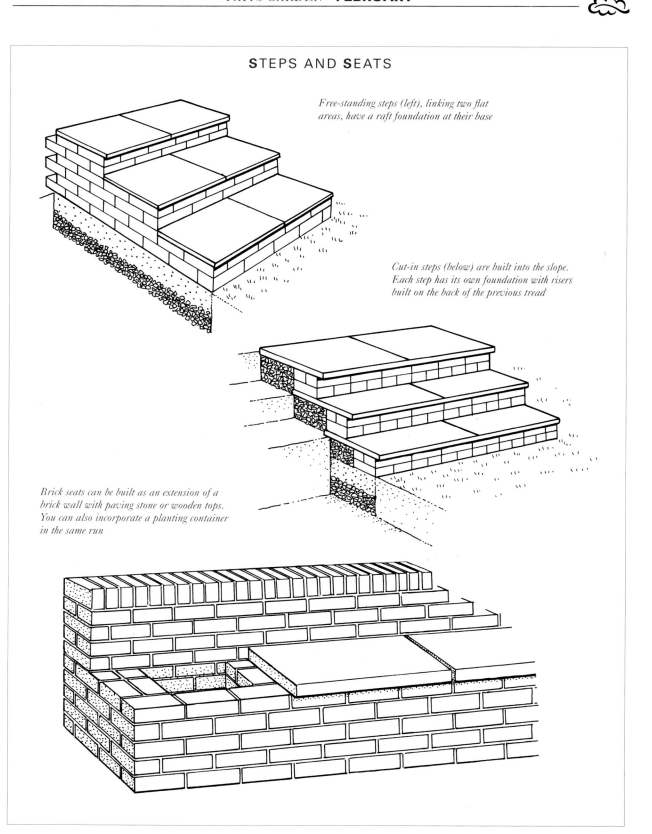

Free-standing steps (left), linking two flat areas, have a raft foundation at their base

Cut-in steps (below) are built into the slope. Each step has its own foundation with risers built on the back of the previous tread

Brick seats can be built as an extension of a brick wall with paving stone or wooden tops. You can also incorporate a planting container in the same run

plants
OF THE
month
2

FIRETHORN
(Pyracantha 'Soleil d'Or')

The pyracanthas are yeoman shrubs of use all round the year. They give evergreen cover, are generous in flower, with frothing masses of creamy blossom in late spring and early summer, and then produce ridiculously heavy crops of berries that are brilliant from the autumn right through the winter till spring.

type	Evergreen shrub
flowers/fruit	Large clusters of small cream flowers cover plants in late spring and early summer. Shining golden berries in large clusters, very persistent from autumn till spring
foliage	Dark green, oval
height	4m (13ft)
spread	4m (13ft)
soil	Not fussy, perhaps best in a deep fertile soil that does not dry out too badly
site	Usually used as a wall shrub for which it is excellent but can be trained up a post, pergola or used as a hedging plant. Best in open sunny spot but will manage well enough in partial shade
care	It is usual to restrict growth by pruning to shape after flowering, tight against wall or other support, but plants in borders can be given free rein save for the removal of ill-placed branches. Check for 'fireblight' which causes cankers at base of dead shoots in autumn. Suspect this bacterial disease if shoots have dead leaves in summer. Cut out all affected branches – preferably 60cm (4in) below affected tissue. Burn prunings and disinfect secateurs
propagation	Semi-ripe cuttings in summer. Plants raised from seed will vary in colour
relatives	There are many firethorns offered, many orange or red as well as gold. *P.* 'Orange Glow' is very reliable; *P.* 'Mohave' is rather richer orange red; *P.* 'Teton' is a prolific, compact, small berried, brilliant old-gold form

HEPATICA
(Hepatica nobilis)

The hepaticas are relatives of the anemones and were once listed in the same genus. They are a choice clan of early flowerers, worth finding a shady, moist, leaf-mouldy spot for.

type	Semi-evergreen perennial
flowers	Wide, open cup-shaped flowers of six or more petals of pale blue; there are dark purple forms, whites and pinks. Late winter and early spring
foliage	Attractive, rounded, rather fleshy leaves, divided into three lobes
height	8cm (3in)
spread	12cm (5in)
soil	Deep soil full of humus such as leaf-mould, preferably rather moist
site	Partial shade where they will not become dried out
care	Resent disturbance so pick the right spot first time
propagation	Intricate roots make it difficult to divide without sacrificing a lot. Pieces can be detached in early spring and replanted and cossetted until re-established. Alternatively, save seed in late spring and sow as soon as harvested
relatives	*H. transsilvanica* is fairly large with a similar range of colour forms

and can have double flowers as can *H. nobilis*. The hybrid *H.* 'Ballardii' is slowish-growing with brilliant blue flowers

CORSICAN HELLEBORE

(Helleborus argutifolius, syn. *H. corsicus)*

One of the best of foliage plants, this perennial could almost be classed as a shrub as although the flowering stems with their leaves die after a year, they will have already have been replaced by new growth. Can be used as bold ground cover.

type	Evergreen perennial
flowers	Large, cornucopia heads of 20 or more bowl-shaped, light apple-green blooms begin to appear with the winter and are in evidence for months
foliage	Tough, spiny toothed, in three leaflets, glossy, veined
height	45cm (18in)
spread	75cm (30in)
soil	Any well-drained soil
site	Border, with shrubs or where it can be left undisturbed
care	Tidy away old stems mid-spring
propagation	Harvest some seed which is borne prolifically and sow in pots or in the open. Plant out seedlings into their permanent site when their first toothed leaf is well developed
relatives	*H. lividus* is closely related but is slightly less hardy. Its leaves are not spiny edged, but its stems, leaves and flowers are flushed purplish pink – a very distinctive and attractive feature and highlighted by the light veining of the leaves

ELEPHANT EARS

(Bergenia × schmidtii)

The bergenias are indestructible ground cover plants. Their foliage can take on red tints in the winter, especially in sunny situations. The huge size of the leaves gives rise to the common name 'elephant ears'.

type	Evergreen, clump-forming perennial
flowers	Generous sprays of many cup-shaped, clean pink flowers on squat stems, late winter to early spring
foliage	Large, oval, tough, dark leaves with serrated margins
height	30cm (12in)
spread	60cm (24in)
soil	Tolerant, best in well-drained soil
site	Sun or shade
care	Remove worn leaves
propagation	Divide in late winter or early autumn
relatives	*B. cordifolia* is similar but a larger beefier plant. *B.* 'Ballawley' has red stems and scarlet flowers, height and spread 60cm (24in)

BAMBOO

(Pleioblastus auricomus, syn. *Arundinaria viridi-striata)*

The bamboos have a marvellous ability to add atmosphere to their surroundings. Perhaps a little expensive, and initially slow to grow, once they have sunk their toes into their new home, they can grow apace and you may need to restrict them. The featured one is slower growing than most.

type	Hardy bamboo
foliage	Conspicuous golden leaves, sometimes with green stripes, on green and purple stems
flowers	Small, inconspicuous grass-like flowers
height	1.5m (5ft)
spread	As allowed
soil	Tolerant
site	Full sun, not very windy
care	Plant firmly in permanent site, limit size of clump by cutting away suckers
propagation	Divide pieces from the main plant in late summer
relatives	*Pleioblastus variegatus* is a dwarf relative up to 80cm (30in) high with narrow green leaves brilliantly striped white. It branches close to the base and is not invasive

practical project 2

PATIO LIGHTING

DIFFERENT SOURCES OF LIGHT

FLOODLIGHTS
Installed high on walls or trees to bathe the whole patio in light. Be careful with the choice of colour; a wall can be given a warmer look with an orange or yellow glow, but the same colour will turn foliage various muddy shades. Make sure you are happy with the floodlit effect as once installed they could be difficult to adjust.

SPOTLIGHTS
Used to highlight a particular plant, container, corner of a raised bed or features such as wall-mounted stone head issuing water. The strength of spots can vary according to the lamp wattage and the distance from the object.

SAFETY LIGHTING
Steps and danger spots such as a pool edge may require a permanent lighting scheme that can be switched on as required. D-I-Y outlets stock a range of waterproof kinds. Do follow installation instructions carefully.

FLARES
They give a live, soft lighting effect. Use only properly manufactured kinds that can be installed securely.

Lighting the patio is an optional extra but it is a temptation that few will resist once everything else is in place. The obvious advantages of lighting include extending the hours when the patio can be used for barbecues or other social occasions. making it safer to move around especially where there are steps and, if linked to a security magic-eye, making the homestead more secure against intruders. When done well lighting can add a theatrical touch, transforming the patio once again.

MAKING CHOICES

There should be no need to take out a second mortgage to finance the lighting. You can make it as simple or elaborate as you wish. A simple system is very effective, particularly in smaller gardens. For larger areas floodlights are useful for illuminating the whole patio and the space around. They can perhaps be used to bring the garden into play as a theatrical stage while leaving the patio less directly lit. Using powerful floodlighting in restricted areas is only really justified as a security measure; if you are sitting on the patio you will feel exposed and vulnerable if lit up as if by a searchlight: the patio is not a football arena or a public utility area! There are lower powered halogen lights that are easy to use, perhaps to illuminate trees or shrubs, or to slant light across the walls of the house with its creepers and attendant plants.

ELECTRIC LIGHTING

Most patios can be lit attractively and adequately by two or three spotlights that highlight certain plants or features but also give plenty of diffused illumination to make sitting, dining and conversing on the patio a pleasant occasion. Inside the house, it is more pleasing if lighting is not too intrusive – outside the same applies. Spots can be used to light up areas where there is activity. For example it is important that the barbecue area is well lighted to avoid accidents – and take account of the possibility of smoke drifting infront of lights and so affecting vision.

While it is possible to make spotlights a movable installation with cables left loose, this may cause trouble, especially with safety. It is far better to spend some time choosing permanent sites for the lights and then use authorized heavy cable buried 38–45cm (15–18in) deep. The heads of the lights are moveable allowing you to change their direction, both before and after installation, giving you versatility should you want to light up a feature directly or bounce some light off a pale surface. View the effects from inside the house as well as from the patio and garden before final fixing.

Manufactured garden lamps mounted on uprights, between 38–45cm (15–18in) high, can be bought as a pack with all the necessary accessories to make installation easy, effective and safe. Such packs include a con-

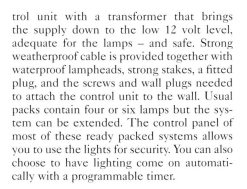

trol unit with a transformer that brings the supply down to the low 12 volt level, adequate for the lamps – and safe. Strong weatherproof cable is provided together with waterproof lampheads, strong stakes, a fitted plug, and the screws and wall plugs needed to attach the control unit to the wall. Usual packs contain four or six lamps but the system can be extended. The control panel of most of these ready packed systems allows you to use the lights for security. You can also choose to have lighting come on automatically with a programmable timer.

FLARES AND CANDLES

Partytime may need extra lights. You could try using strings of coloured bulbs that are often seen decorating garden entrances at Christmas. They can look very effective carefully strung over the patio. Only use ones designed for outdoors with proper cable, connections and with a current breaker.

If in the slightest doubt get a qualified electrician to install the lighting or at least check your work before switching on.

Garden flares or candles can be used for temporary lighting. They can be positioned among foliage and flowers of plants and lit when you are ready. The flares give a soft glow that is most attractive, however the amount of light they provide is not enormous and they are best as a supplement to your powered permanent lighting. A little commonsense is worth using when siting these flares; no breeze should be able to move the flame too near any plant or inflammable object – including guests – and use only properly manufactured flares.

PLANTS TO LIGHT FOR DRAMATIC EFFECT

Aralia elata 'Variegata'
Birches, various including *Betula utilis jacquemontii*
Catalpa bignonioides
C.b. 'Aurea'
Cordyline australis
Eucalyptus, various
Hostas
Yuccas

Also consider any water features

MARCH

There is no doubt about it, the bulbs are well underway, almonds and
forsythias take over the stage. This must be spring.

Some of the berried shrubs of winter still display their fruit, although
the main winter-flowering shrubs are over. Witch hazels are bare-
stemmed but leaf buds are swelling and beginning to break before the
month's end. Those shrubs that straddle winter and spring, the hazels
and willows, may be flowering freely, as may Corylopsis pauciflora,
with its unusual catkins, and C. spicata – probably at their best this
month with pale-coloured blossom and the latter delighting also with
its sweet scent. In the coolest months, it is difficult to imagine what
insects the winter flowers hope to tempt with their scents, but now there
are bees and other insects on the wing when the sun shines. Heathers
can be buzzing with visitors.

Birds are busy building nests and marking their territories with song.
The less melodious song of the male frogs advertizing mating activity
may be audible; the garden pond may already reveal frog spawn.
Toads and newts usually wait a little longer. Other less pleasing
forms of life – slugs and snails – are now in a period of
hyperactivity. Now is the time to try to get the numbers of these
creatures under control. With seeds germinating and potted plants
beginning to grow, gardeners are preparing to be busy, but there is
still time to contemplate major construction works in the garden
before plant activities claim our time.

tasks
FOR THE
month

CHECKLIST

- Planting shrubs and climbers
- Summer-flowering bulbs
- Checking rock beds
- Hygiene of raised beds
- Woodwork maintenance
- Tending ivies

PLANTING SHRUBS AND CLIMBERS

Early this month is one of the best times to plant shrubs and climbers. Normally there is plenty of rainfall and the warming soils will help roots to grow energetically and to get the whole established soundly.

There are a variety of site types around the patio, including the house walls (see project p.140), places near the wall that benefit from its warmth, raised beds on or by the patio, the more traditional beds leading into the garden and finally those parts of the main garden viewed from the patio.

Planting
- Ensure that the specimen to be planted has its rootstock thoroughly watered.

- Excavate a ten pound hole

for a one pound plant; this means that the soil below and around the planted specimen will be worked to encourage easy rooting.

- Dig over the bottom of the hole, incorporating rubble and drainage material where needed; against a wall it may be more important to add moisture-retaining humus in almost any form.

- Have a supply of good healthy topsoil ready for returning around the newly-placed plant.

- Place a stake in if necessary.

- Tease out and spread any pot-bound roots.

- Plant firmly and water in thoroughly.

- Trim any broken twigs.

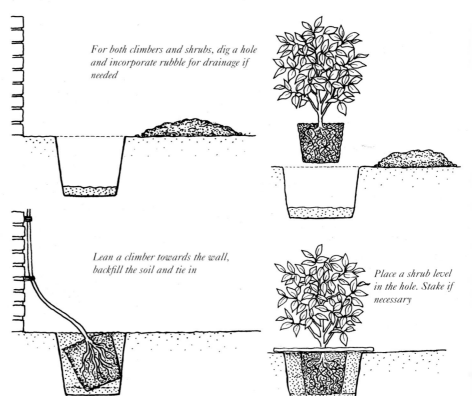

For both climbers and shrubs, dig a hole and incorporate rubble for drainage if needed

Lean a climber towards the wall, backfill the soil and tie in

Place a shrub level in the hole. Stake if necessary

SUMMER-FLOWERING BULBS

The main summer bulb is the lily, but there are also a number of others that are sometimes overlooked including the half-hardy kinds, such as the smaller gladioli, sparaxis, tigridias and ixias. These will have been for sale for some weeks in the garden centres. They can now be planted out to bloom *in situ*, earlier they could have been put into pots (see p.22) to start them off before planting out the growing potfuls when frosts are likely to be past. (See margin for suggestions.)

CHECKING ROCK BEDS

Spring is the busiest time here with lots of the small plants of mountain tops and elsewhere getting into bloom. It may be time to tidy around, making sure that any rocks have not got dislodged and loose after winter frosts. Mulches or top-dressings of rock chips or gravel may need freshening up either with a thin scattering or with new material.

First go over the bed and remove any weeds — look carefully for any seedlings around your pet plants; they may be having babies which you can transplant elsewhere.

HYGIENE OF RAISED BEDS

Raised beds used for a mix of bulbs, shrubs and bedding plants can be worked over now after removing loose, dead material to the compost heap. If the soil mix seems healthy — and the plants will be the best indication of this — all you need to do is to fork over after scattering a little general fertilizer. Check that drainage is working efficiently as well. If soil appears sodden, chip away any blocked drainage holes and replace overheavy soil with recommended compost as used for pots (p.41).

BUYING SHRUBS

BARE-ROOT TREES AND SHRUBS
At the beginning of this month a few places will be selling bare-root shrubs. They are usually much cheaper than container plants and will have an extensive root system. Buy as early as possible, keep the roots moist, and plant firmly then water thoroughly. These plants can sometimes get away to a better start than container plants.

CONTAINER SHRUB AND TREES
Don't
- *Buy specimens that have been cut back one or more times, usually easily recognized by the broad pruning cuts*
- *Get specimens that are heavily root-bound and have obviously been this way for some considerable time*

Do
- *Look for healthy foliage*
- *Make sure the base of the shrub is not riding high in the container soil*
- *If buying roses make sure that the root tops are not exposed*
- *Consider buying younger, smaller samples which may be a better bet than ones that have been living in the containers for a long time*
- *Make sure your choice is appropriate for its site so that you do not plant a fat cuckoo in a robin's nest*
- *Check plant labels for height, but these are not always very accurate*

WOODWORK MAINTENANCE

Before other jobs claim your attention, check paintwork to see whether you need to apply a fresh coat anywhere. Examine the timber of pergolas and other features for rot and to make sure they are secure. Give a coat of preservative if necessary, but take note of the manufacturer's instructions and the possibility of toxicity to plants.

TENDING IVIES

Give ivies an extra gloss by encouraging the growth of fresh clean leaves, especially where plants are in a conspicuous position such as against a wall, up a post or over a shed. Simply strip off a lot of the older foliage with shears or a mechanical cutter.

BULBS FOR PLANTING NOW

Allium cernuum, purplish pink, Ht. 30cm (12in)
Crocosmia (**montbretia**), various including:
C. '**Lucifer**', red, Ht. 90cm (36in)
C. masonorum, orange, Ht. 1.5m (5ft)
Galtonia candicans, white, Ht. 60–90cm (24–36in)
G. viridflora, pale green, Ht. 1–1.2m (3–4ft)
Gladiolus communis byzantinus, hardy, maroon-pink Ht. 90cm (36in)
G. Primulinus hybrids, semi-hardy, various colours, Ht. 1–1.2m (3-4ft)
G. Nanus hybrids, hardy near walls, various colours, Ht. 30–50cm (12–20in)
Ixia, all colours, half-hardy, Ht. 30–40cm (12–15in)
Lilies, all types
Nerine bowdenii, pink, autumn-flowering, Ht. 38–45cm (15–18in)
Sparaxis tricolor, half-hardy, orange, red, purple Ht. 15–30cm (6–12in)
Tigridia, many colours, half-hardy, Ht. 30cm (12in)

POTTED BULBS AND TULIPS

Further pots of spring bulbs can be brought out in succession as they begin to look interesting – perhaps buds showing their first flash of colour. Top the surfaces with a handful of peat, shredded bark or gravel to give a neat appearance. They are now on stage and should look their best.

plants
OF THE
month
1

▲ CAMELLIA
(Camellia 'Donation'*)*

Camellias are evergreen shrubs that look shiny-new and handsome at all times. They do best in neutral or acid soil but can be grown well in tubs where lime is prevalent. *C.* 'Donation' is exceptionally free-flowering. Although the plant is hardy the flowers can be frosted so a sheltered site is advisable.

type	Evergreen shrub
flowers	Large semi-double, rich pink, round flowers; winter into spring
foliage	Dark tough oval leaves, quite shiny
height	3m (10ft)
spread	Eventually 3m (10ft)
soil	Healthy, neutral to acid
site	Best sheltered from frost. Excellent with other shrubs near a wall or in a warm shrub border
care	Do not allow it to suffer drought, remove faded flowers
propagation	Summer cuttings or layers
relatives	*C.* 'Caerhays' has larger leaves, an arching habit and rather variable semi-double flowers often with anemone-type centres, crimson-pink becoming mauvy with age

◀ WANDA PRIMROSES
(Primula juliae Wanda Primroses*)*

Do not confuse this strain with the old 'Wanda' cultivar; though these have similar neat habit and bloom prolifically and early, they have rather larger flowers and are multi-coloured. Plants are robust, forming dense clumps.

type	Herbaceous perennial
flowers	Many pink, red, mauve or purple, flat primrose blooms making a low mound; early to mid-spring
foliage	Wrinkled, polished dark purple-green leaves, the size of wild primrose now, but only very small over winter
height	10cm (4in)
spread	25cm (10in) spread
soil	Not fussy
site	Borders, large containers, rock gardens
care	Lift and split every two years, discarding older centre pieces
propagation	See care. Also sow seed as soon as ripe
relatives	*P.* 'Tawny Port' is an older hybrid with port-coloured blossom

LENTEN ROSES
(Helleborus orientalis)

While these can start flowering in the autumn and through the winter, now they are in high season. The flower sizes, forms and colours of good modern hybrids are so splendid as to make them everyone's favourites. They are especially useful as long-term tenants of shady or semi-shady spots near the patio.

type	Herbaceous evergreen perennial
flowers	White, cream, primrose, mauve, purple or almost black, with or without spots; winter and spring
foliage	Tough, dark green leaflets arranged like palms. See care
height	45cm (18in)
spread	45cm (18in)
soil	Not fussy, but likes deep soils
site	Enjoys semi-shade
care	Plant and leave undisturbed except to propagate. Established plants can have leaves cut away and burnt at year end. This makes blossom much easier to see and enjoy and will reduce the chance of black fungus attack
propagation	At flowering time, just before new leaves emerge, lift clump and carefully divide crown, with each division having plenty of root, replant immediately and keep moist. Sow seed as soon as ripe
relatives	It is most economical to buy unnamed seedlings of good strains. Named cultivars are expensive. Be careful – high demand leads to inferior kinds being sold

▼ RHODODENDRON
(Rhododendron × praecox)

This extremely popular old hybrid, resulting from a cross between *R. cilatum* and *R. dauricum*, is compact in growth. It is semi-evergreen, losing its leaves in hard winters. The attractive flowers are very freely produced.

type	Semi-evergreen shrub
flowers	Clusters of three, rosy-mauve, funnel-shaped; late winter to early spring
foliage	Dark, oval, small, 5–8cm (2–3in) long
height	1–1.4m (3–5ft)
spread	1–1.4m (3–5ft)
soil	Well-drained, neutral to acid
site	Not fussy
care	Keep weeded; do not let larger bushes overcrowd it
propagation	Air layering
relatives	*R.* 'Tessa', from *R. praecox × moupinense*, has more open flowers in paler pink

practical project 1

CONSIDERING CONTAINERS

POT SHAPES AND SIZES

- The smaller the container the sooner it dries out
- Larger containers will be immovable once filled with compost and plants
- Square pots contain far more compost than round ones of the same diameter
- Linear measurements are of the interior diameter of a round pot or of one side of a plastic one
- A pot is the same depth as its diameter
- A half-pot is half the depth of its diameter
- A pan is one third the depth of its diameter
- Plastic pots are often slightly wider than deep and are usually manufactured to take a certain volume of compost.

  2 litre = 14.5 x 14.5cm (5¹/₂ x 5¹/₂in)

  3 litre = 18 x15.4cm (7 x 6in)

  4 litre = 20 x 20cm (8 x 8in)

  5 litre = 23 x 23cm (9 x 9in)

  10 litre = 28 x 22cm (11 x 9in)

Confronted with the huge range of containers of different materials, styles and sizes it is easy to get bewildered and diffident when choosing. However, there are a few simple ways in which to narrow down your choice.

MATERIAL

Earthenware Terracotta colours are warm and any raw newness soon mellows. The material breathes and with good drainage holes earthenware containers can be many gardeners' first choice. Clay pots around 20cm (8in) and similar sized containers are the smallest really feasible. 15cm (6in) ones can only really be contemplated if sunk within a larger container in peat or other material that will keep the pots cool and moist.

Plastic Utilitarian but also sometimes decorative. Easily cleaned and moisture preserving, plastic containers can look correct in a modern setting. Avoid overcomplicated shapes or ornamentation; better to be simple and let the plants do the decorative bit.

Stoneware Both true stone or reconstituted material can look very good. New stone soon takes on the patina of age. You do not need to buy stone which has been sprayed with paint to give it a false patina. Stone and earthenware artifacts mix well. (See project p.44 and think about making your own.)

Metal Stately homes may display centuries-old lead and other solid metal containers, but these are in the 'old masters' price range. There are modern reproductions but these too are pricey. Metal containers have the advantage of long life and are probably of a substantial size with good drainage facilities.

Wood Half barrels can last a considerable time. Each can certainly support a considerable slice of plant life as they hold a large amount of compost. Normally they have to be permanently sited; to move them means emptying them first. Versailles box-shaped containers have become fashionable and have a more classical look than the half barrels. Wooden windowboxes are best in a simple design.

Hanging baskets and cradles These are metal or plastic. Small hanging baskets are difficult to manage; those below 25cm (10in) are really too small (see also project p.64). Cradles made of substantial metal can be large enough to contain a lot of growing medium and support a miniature garden.

DEPLOYING CONTAINERS

There is not much room for mistakes when placing permanent containers. They are obviously going to be focal points but must not jeopardize the use of the patio for sitting and dining. Planted carefully, troughs with miniature gardens of alpines can look well all round the year. Some pots can be decorative in themselves, without the extra colour of plants. Stoneware has a look of permanence and classical urns look well in a formal setting. These are usually of sufficient size as to take substantial plants perhaps shrubs or examples of topiary or, if year round colour is not vital, a group of larger herbaceous items such as agapanthus or hostas.

One large earthenware container can look good – empty or full. However, a group of three looks more than three times as impressive. Movable containers allow a useful degree of flexibility. They allow the patio to be viewed as a stage. Here is where the action is. Have a succession of containers planted up with permanent or ephemeral plant life and keep them in the wings until they develop enough to be wheeled out just as they become really interesting. (See project p.120).

PLANTING

Plants in containers are restricted in their search for nutrients and water: all containers, even the largest, have finite amounts of rooting medium so it must be of the best quality and it must be kept as healthy as possible with good drainage to avoid waterlogging.

Procedure

- Make sure drainage holes are sufficient and if need be add extra or enlarge existing ones.
- Cover drainage holes with perforated plastic or metal to allow free drainage but stop slugs or other small creatures entering.
- Fill with a good potting compost with added fertilizer (see below).

Potting mix

A basic potting mix can be made up of the following ingredients by volume:

2 healthy loam (rotted grass turf for example)

1¹/₂ peat or humus such as leafmould

1 washed sand or grit

This is not far removed from the John Innes potting compost recipe but favours a higher proportion of humus, which not only helps feed plants, but is important in retaining moisture and the air-rich structure that is so vital. If not making your own mix, purchase John Innes and add a little extra humus.

Slow-release fertilizer capsules are recommended as they work for the whole growing season and should support healthy growth without needing extra back-up.

Planting a strawberry pot/planter

■ Choose as large a container as possible, checking that the planting pockets are large enough to work with.

■ Place the pot in its permanent site and raise it on bricks or drainage feet; if there is no drainage hole in the bottom carefully drill one at least 2cm (1in) wide.

■ Cover inside base with a layer of gravel about 5cm (2in) deep.

■ Place a length of drainage pipe 7–10cm (3–4in) wide to stand upright in the centre.

■ Fill with compost such as John Innes No 1 or 2 around the pipe. Fill pipe with gravel and pull the pipe up as the soil level rises to leave a centre drainage core through the compost. Remove the pipe when within 15cm (6in) from top and make the whole of the top level of pure compost.

■ You can plant in pockets as you fill the pot with soil or when it is full. It is a little easier to get roots spread out to plant while filling.

■ At the top, finish planting with about three spreading plants. Leave room for watering.

Incorporating a much perforated plastic pipe reaching up from the bottom of the pot to the soil surface as you fill it with compost will aid internal watering. Be prepared to rejig the pot each spring with fresh plants or propagated pieces and fresh compost.

PLASTIC V TERRACOTTA

PLASTIC
■ **Cheap**
■ **Light, therefore easy to handle but not so stable**
■ **Easily cleaned**
■ **Impervious so retains moisture longer**

TERRACOTTA
■ **Attractive appearance**
■ **Weighty and so more stable, especially with larger sizes and plants**
■ **Porosity helps drainage and helps prevent sodden conditions**
■ **More difficult to clean**
■ **Costs more**

A length of drainage pipe inserted in the centre and filled with gravel enables easy watering. If the pipe is much perforated it can be left in place once the pot is full

Suitable plants for your strawberry pot – apart from repeat-fruiting strawberries – include a wide selection of herbs such as lemon verbena, thymes, sages, chives. These can be mixed in with lobelia and other strictly decorative items

plants
OF THE
month
2

▼ SIBERIAN BUGLOSS
(Brunnera macrophylla)

I cannot ever remember hearing this plant's 'common' name being used: it looks more forget-me-not than bugloss! An easy plant, it can cope with a dryish spot and will be happy with some shade. Leaves expand after the long flowering period to make a foliage plant almost as bold as a hosta.

type	Herbaceous perennial
flowers	Many sky-blue, forget-me-nots in loose wide sprays of fine stems for many weeks through spring
foliage	Heart-shaped, rough-textured, grey-green leaves making thick cover are small when blooming starts but up to 25cm (20in) long later
height	45cm (18in)
spread	60cm (24in)
soil	Any, moist to dryish
site	Open or semi-shaded
care	Easy plant. Remove dead leaves at year's end
propagation	By seed. It will probably give its own offerings of self-sown seedlings
relatives	*B. macrophylla* 'Dawsons White', syn. *B.m.* 'Variegata', has the same small flowers and habit as the type but the leaves are boldly and attractively margined in cream

JONQUIL DAFFODILS
(Narcissus 'Sun Disc'*)*

A few bulbs of this dwarf jonquil hybrid will produce a surprising quantity of perfect blooms a little later than *N.* 'February Gold' (see above). It has erect, neat, narrow foliage, rating a low score on the nuisance scale. Bulbs increase rapidly and will make themselves at home in a warm spot by the patio or in a container. Only lightly perfumed.

type	Bulb
flowers	Very circular, bright yellow with a flat disc-like crown, 4cm (1½in) across. Very free of bloom. Mid- to late spring
foliage	Narrow, erect
height	15–20cm (6–8in)
soil	Well-drained
site	Open to light
care	Easy, fast increasing bulb best lifted, split and replanted every second year in early summer
propagation	See care

relatives N. 'Sundial' is similar, often with two rather smaller flowers to a stem

CYCLAMINEUS DAFFODILS

▼ *(Narcissus* 'February Gold'*)*

N. 'February Gold' is a trusted *N. cyclamineus* hybrid, but in fact all the offspring of this species are ideal patio plants. They come into bloom early, and are very persistent and weatherproof in bloom. Their size is right and their foliage being much less than that of larger hybrids is more easily managed as it dies down.

type Bulb
flowers Golden with pointed petals very slightly reflexed from the long cup; long lasting; late winter to early spring
foliage Erect, grey green

height 25–30cm (10–12in)
soil Not fussy
site Pots, containers, troughs, the rock garden, between shrubs, in borders or grass. Outstanding naturalized
care Plant with 10cm (4in) of soil over the bulb noses in late summer or early autumn
propagation Lift and split in early summer
relatives All Cyclamineus narcissus are excellent garden plants. *N.* 'Tête à Tête' and *N.* 'Jumblie' are even earlier and only half the height, their flowers last over six weeks. *N.* 'Jenny' is similar in height to *N.* 'February Gold', but with more recurving, pointed white petals and slender trumpets, opening primrose and becoming white

LEOPARD'S BANE ▲

(Doronicum orientale 'Gold Dwarf'*)*

Presumably to be recommended for keeping leopards out of the garden, doronicums are usually tall border plants but this kind is dwarf – very dwarf when it first starts to bloom. It can be relied on for plenty of golden blossom through the early weeks and months of the year. The foliage is not too dominant after blooming and a clump close to the patio edge need not be an empty spot later – other plants can be planted to overlap it.

type Herbaceous perennial
flowers Golden daisies 5–6cm (2–2¹/₂in) across, through spring
foliage Light green, serrated heart-shaped, very small at beginning of flowering time, not too large later. Insignificant after midsummer
height 15–20cm (6–8in)
spread 20–25cm (8–10in)
soil Any
site Open, border or bed
care Very easy plant
propagation By division of fat surface rhizomes after flowering or in late summer
relatives Most are tall and better away from the patio. *D. orientale* 'Spring Beauty' makes good clumps and has well-doubled flowers of gold on stems 30–45cm (12–18in) high

A sunny splash of colour on the patio: Doronicum orientale *(left) with trollius*

practical project 2

MAKING TROUGHS AND CONTAINERS

SUGGESTED ALPINES FOR TROUGHS

Androsace carnea, pink
A. sempervivoides, pink
A. villosa jacquemontii, pink
Arenaria balearica, white
A. purpurascens, pink
Armeria juniperifolia, pink
Dianthus alpinus and all the smaller more compact kinds
Draba aizoides, yellow
D. rigida imbricata, yellow
Gentiana saxosa, white
G. verna, vivid blue
Potentilla neumanniana nana, gold
Primula marginata, mauve
P. pubescens, in variety, white, pink, mauve, purple
Saxifragas – especially Kabschia kinds
Saxifraga 'Wisley', maroon
Sedums – the tidier less rampant ones
Sempervivums
Wahlenbergia pumilio, blue

Nowadays, genuine old stone troughs are very much collectors' pieces and are auctioned by firms that also deal in million pound paintings. Rock garden enthusiasts find these ideal for growing their precious little plants, provided they are not less than 15cm (6in) deep and have drainage holes. If you win the lottery, go for the genuine article, otherwise, follow the instructions below and you have a real chance of fooling the experts.

The usual plan is to reproduce an old stone trough such as were used for centuries by farmers. However, you do not need to restrict yourself to conventional oblong forms; your containers could be round, oval or even roughly triangular. Larger ones could have five, six or more sides. Manufacturing principles are the same.

SIZE AND FORM

■ Plants need a good root run: make sure inner depths are not less than 15cm (6in), but preferably 20cm (8in). If you are making more than one, it adds variety to have various depths up to 38–45cm (15–18in).
■ Do not make any too small. The smallest ought to be able to take as much soil as contained by a 20cm (8in) pot.
■ Do not make any too large to move.
■ Any trough with dimensions larger than the equivalent of 35 x 60 x 20cm (14 x 24 x 8in) should be reinforced by incorporating crushed chicken wire within the mix. Make sure that the wire does not protrude to the surfaces.

THE STONE

The 'stone' is made of a material often called hypertufa – tufa being a soft strataless rock. It is made of the following material mixed by volume:

2 of sieved moist sphagnum peat or similar humus material
1 of sand/fine grit
1 of cement

This will end up as a grey stone; if you want a colour you can add yellow, red or orange colourants in amounts as recommended by manufacturers. A rather garish rich initial new colour will soon tone down to something very much more mellow, but still warmer than the straightforward grey; however, the uncoloured stone will take on its own colouring as moss and lichen take hold – something that can happen quickly.

MAKING THE TROUGH

Make moulds for whatever shape you have chosen. Straight-sided ones are possibly easier than rounded ones as you can use either wood or strong cardboard. Rounded ones can be made easily enough using strong cardboard or strips of hardboard. You need to make an outer and an inner mould; the dimensions of the inner one allowing for a gap of 4–5cm (1½–2in) all round and below.

Wooden moulds can be used many times. The outer mould need only be four sided with no base. Joined by screws, these will be easier to remove from the completed container. Both moulds can be made just a touch narrower at the base than the top; it will certainly pay to ensure that the inner mould is just 1–2cm (½–1in) narrower at the bottom so that it is pulled clear of the whole more easily when the mix has set. Run over the outer surfaces of the inner mould and the inner surface of the outer mould with rough sand/emery paper to remove any small projection or wisps of wood that could get set in the mix.

Remember drainage holes. Dummy holes can be made of wood plugs or cardboard rolls stuffed with paper. Make holes 3cm (1–1½in) wide and 4–5cm (1½–2in) deep to allow for the thickness of the bottom of the container.

Procedure
■ Place the outer mould in position. Place baseless wooden ones on even soil or sand. Support the sides of cardboard ones with soil or sand so that they do not give completely when wet and under pressure from the weight of the mix.

■ Mix 'stone' ingredients thoroughly to a wet but not loose consistency.

■ Place drainage plugs in position, perhaps some 7cm (3in) from each corner.

■ Introduce mix until 4–5cm (1½–2in) deep, ie level with the top of the plugs. (Remember with large containers to use chicken wire reinforcing in base and up the sides.)

■ Put the inner mould in place using a brick

or two to weigh it down and prevent movement.

■ Work mix around sides, making sure no air holes are left.

■ When complete, cover with a damp sack or sheet of polythene and leave for a few days steady drying.
■ Carefully remove the outer mould.

■ Rub down any sharp edges without trying to get an artificially smooth surface.

■ Replace cover and leave for a few more drying days – perhaps a week or even longer.

■ Remove the inner mould and drainage plugs; smooth down any sharp edges

■ Move to permanent quarters and raise a few centimetres above ground level on slates, bricks or stones. Ensure that it is stable.

The cardboard moulds will give a bit during the construction to produce a slightly uneven surface – altogether a very natural feature, especially when any sharp projections are smoothed down

Once in place the containers are ready for filling with soil and planting (see margins for suggested alpines – although you could fill them with bedding plants if you prefer). Use compost mix similar to that for pots (see p.41).

If you want to encourage a quick growth of moss and algae on the surfaces, they can be painted with a sloppy mix of yogurt, sour milk or cow manure.

MINI TREES AND SHRUBS FOR TROUGHS

Conifers
***Abies balsamea* 'Hudsonia'**
***A. balsamea* 'Nana'**
***Chamaecyparis obtusa* 'Nana Gracilis'**
***C. pisifera* 'Nana'**
***Juniperus communis* 'Compressa'**

SHRUBS

Genista sagittalis delphinensis, very dwarf broom with wings along twigs
Hebe, many small, evergreen
Helichrysum coralloides, tiny, striped, erect
***Ilex crenata* 'Mariesii',** miniature holly
Jasminum parkeri, little dark green, intricate shrub, yellow flowers
Salix × boydii, upright, round-leaved willow
S. reticulata, prostrate willow with shiny, round leaves
Thymus, the erect ones, some with gold- and silver-variegation

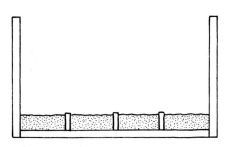

Position the smaller mould inside the larger one and add hypertufa down the sides

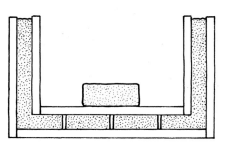

Fill the base of the larger mould with hypertufa and insert wooden dowels for drainage holes

Dismantle the outer mould once the mix has set

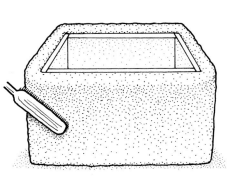

Roughen the outside for a more authentic effect

APRIL

More than most, this month is a mixed programme of weather: bright
sunshine and warm weather one minute and showers the next, with the
odd frost at night. Frosts may cut back some of the more adventurous
of the new growth but such natural pruning is usually more evident
away in the garden rather than near the patio and house, where brick,
stone and additional shelter normally retains a reserve of warmth
and protection that protects the inhabitants' growth.

Perhaps shrubs and trees that have been flowering through winter and
early spring are now singing their blossom swansong, but they will
soon be making vigorous foliage and stem growth. The winter-
flowering cherry, Prunus subhirtella autumnalis may scatter a flurry
of petals among the unfurling new foliage and, more certainly, the
Chaenomeles against the house walls will decorate its branches
generously with flowers and fresh leaves: red and green patterns from
C. 'Knap Hill Scarlet', pink and green from C. 'Appleblossom', and
white and green from C. 'Nivalis'.

Often, climbers on walls and scrambling along pergolas are the first to
show signs of vigorous new activity; by this month honeysuckles can be
leafy and small-flowered Clematis montana is beginning its gushing
displays. Even wisterias may be tempted to produce their first
blossoms, although they sometimes hold back and are without leaf or
flower until next month. The rock bed close to the patio and the trough
garden planted up with alpines is now at its most exciting and
generous. Every plant, big or little, seems intent on outdoing its
neighbour in floral endeavour.

On warm days it is tempting to sit outside and enjoy the private Eden.
Why not? The garden and patio are for enjoyment. Turn a blind eye,
for a moment, to the jobs that beckon in the garden. The weeds are not
too big or threatening yet, tomorrow is time enough to bring out the hoe
and do gentle battle.

tasks
FOR THE
month

**PELARGONIUMS
(GERANIUMS)**

**For most gardeners' purposes
these plants fall into the following
categories:**

Zonal geraniums – the bedding
types which are now
commonly sold as strains
raised from seed
Ivy-leaved geraniums – with
pointed, ivy-like leaves and
available as miniature, dwarf
and standard
Trailing geraniums – which
includes some ivy-leaved ones
Scented-leaved geraniums –
perfumed when touched.
Lemon-scented is particularly
prevalent

CHECKLIST

- ☐ Potting on
- ☐ Checking pelargoniums
- ☐ Watering plans
- ☐ Hardening bedding plants
- ☐ Checking garden furniture

POTTING ON

Everything is growing fast
now. Roots are very active
and this makes it the ideal
time for moving potted plants
into slightly larger containers
and introducing fresh
compost so that growth is not
impeded. The opportunity can
be taken to give the plants a
dose of fertilizer – a general
one, such as Growmore, or
some slow-release capsules.
Seedlings of bedding plants
should be growing on with as
little check as possible.

■ From seed pots or trays,
prick them out into new trays,
spacing them about 5cm (2in)
apart.

■ Seedlings growing in trays
divided into modules suffer
less root disturbance and by
now these plants could be
ready for a final move into
larger individual quarters.

■ Tenderer ones perhaps into
hanging baskets and other
such containers under
glass.

■ Hardier ones into

containers on site or into
flower beds.

■ Water before moving the
seedlings and, as far as
possible, avoid root loss or
disturbance then water again.

■ A sheet of polythene or
even newspaper covering the
newly-homed seedlings for a
day or so can help in hot,
sunny spells.

CHECKING PELARGONIUMS

Overwintered pelargoniums
(geraniums) will have started
into growth some weeks ago
after an almost complete
drought in their frost-proof
winter sites. Now they are
growing fast. Slow-release
fertilizer in the compost used
for potting up the plants will
suffice for most of the
season. It is a mistake to
feed too much nitrogen and
grow large healthy plants,
which just produce a cloud of
leaves. Once pelargoniums
have got going they can be
kept moderately starved and
they do not need the copious
amounts of water required by
many other plants — being a
little hungry and a touch
thirsty encourages bud
formation. The aim is to have
the plants showing flower by
next month when they can be
planted out.

WATERING PLANS

Much of the success of the
living part of the patio
depends on the supply of
water. Hanging baskets and
containers will dry out quickly
due to the weather and the
transpiration rates of the
crowded busily growing
plants. Although watering
needs can be fulfilled with a
ready watering can,
especially if there is a
conveniently placed water
butt nearby, life can be made
a little easier with some

simple irrigation systems.

Trickle irrigation can be provided via narrow piping and small valves. A valve is placed in each hanging basket and is adjusted to give a steady but small supply of dripping water. The amount of water passing is not great but each atom is getting where it is needed – down at the roots – and almost none is lost to straightforward evaporation. Link the narrow gauge piping to the mains supply via a non-return valve. It is possible to install a timing device to have the water supply come on for a limited period each day. (See also practical project p.64 and tasks p.86.)

Small plastic bottles can also be used to make watering easier. Cut off the top third to a half of the bottle, make plenty of small holes in it and then insert it upside down in the compost as you plant up the container. The holes ensure water can percolate around the roots. This method is especially useful for hanging baskets that are hung above head height.

HARDENING BEDDING PLANTS

Bedding plants luxuriating in the closeted comfort of a warm, moist greenhouse or conservatory cannot be introduced directly to the garden-proper without risk of disaster. They need the halfway house of a cold frame or sheltered area where they can become more slowly accustomed to the realities of life in the open. If in a cold frame give them daily increases of air; if in a sheltered spot make sure

they are protected at night and during bad weather. If severe frosts are threatened the frame tops or plastic coverings must be secured.

CHECKING GARDEN FURNITURE

If this has not been done already it is high time to get the furniture out and make sure that it is all serviceable and clean.

Wooden furniture may be in need of a gentle facelift with some wood preservative or light oil.

MORE LILIES

Lilies are well worth reconsidering this month, perhaps with a new selection to pot up. Oriental kinds such as *L.* 'Star Gazer' and *L.* 'Journey's End' bloom later and may be at their best late summer and early autumn. Not only are they spectacular in bloom but have a huge perfume. (More ideas and planting procedure are given on p.13.)

ASIATIC HYBRIDS
Any available now, perhaps:
L. 'Connecticut King', yellow, 75cm (30in)
L. 'Cote d'Azur', upward-facing, rich pink, 45–60cm (18–24in)
L. 'Enchantment', orange, 75cm (30in)
L. 'Medaillon', upward-facing, creamy yellow, 1m (3ft)
L. 'Mont Blanc', upward-facing, white, 75cm (30in)
L. Pixies, (see p.13)
L. 'Yellow Blaze', upward-facing, gold with dark spots, 1.2m (4ft)

ORIENTAL HYBRIDS
L. 'Casa Blanca', outward-facing, white, 1.2m (4ft)
L. 'Journey's End', outward-facing, crimson, late, 1.5m (5ft)
L. 'La Reve', completely pink, 75cm (30in)
L. 'Mona Lisa', outward-facing, pink, 50–75cm (20–30in)
L. 'Mr Edd', white, 30cm (12in)
L. 'Mr Rud', white and gold, 30cm (12in)
L. 'Mr Sam', pink and white edges, 30cm (12in)
L. 'Star Gazer', upward-facing, white-edged crimson, 1.2m (4ft)
L. 'Sublime', white and yellow with tiny maroon dots, 30cm (12in)

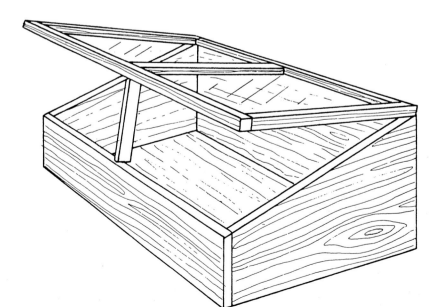

plants
OF THE
month
1

HYACINTH
(Hyacinthus orientalis 'Delft Blue'*)*

How many millions of hyacinth bulbs get potted up each year to be coaxed into early bloom? A lot, and too many rather unsuccessfully. Outside they are easier to manage. I find the blue kinds the strongest and although fat new bulbs produce sturdy, more crowded blossom, the second or third year stems with their florets more widely spaced look more naturally graceful.

type	Bulb
flowers	Pale blue base, much overpainted with darker violet-blue; highly fragrant; unprepared bulbs are in bloom now
foliage	Polished, strap-shaped, almost erect, short at flowering time but growing longer after
height	20cm (8in)
soil	Open, with some humus
site	Containers, raised beds, borders
care	Outside plant in late summer to early autumn with 8cm (4in) soil over top of the bulbs. In containers plant as early as possible and cover with at least 5cm (2in) soil
propagation	If bulbs are left to die down naturally, lift after 2 or 3 years and split clumps
relatives	H. 'Ostara', dark blue; H. 'Blue Magic', deep blue with white eye; H. 'Carnegie', white; H. 'City of Haarlem', pale primrose; H. 'Gypsy Queen', apricot; H. 'Lady Derby', pale pink; H. 'Hollyhock', double, red

MONTANA CLEMATIS
(Clematis montana rubens)

Of all the small-flowered clematis, this must be top favourite; it grows so easily and quickly, will manage in all sorts of situations and will unfailingly come up trumps each spring with crowded galaxies of bloom. The only attention it needs is to cut back growth where it is spreading beyond its allotted space.

type	Deciduous climber
flowers	Four oblong petals to each of the countless pink blooms, early to mid-spring for several weeks
foliage	In three-lobed leaflets, green but flushed pink
height	8–12m (25–40ft)
spread	3m (10ft) but can travel for long distances along branches or pergolas
soil	Not fussy as long as it has decent drainage
site	Best in open but can grow through trees and shrubs to come out on top
care	Only needs to have excess growth cut back
propagation	By layers or cuttings
relatives	There are a series of C. montana forms: the type is white, C. montana 'Tetrarose' is a bolder plant with larger leaflets and flowers of satin pink, half as big again as the type. C. montana 'Elizabeth' is a popular, good form with widely spaced petals of shining pink

FORCING HYACINTHS

Hyacinths may also be forced from late autumn for early flowering, perhaps to be displayed on the patio on mild winter days or to be brought into the house. Use prepared bulbs and a bowl with drainage holes and a saucer. Fill bowl loosely with bulb fibre or peat-based compost and place bulbs in position, 3 to a 15–20cm (6–8in) bowl. Do not compress compost below bulbs.

- Water thoroughly and allow to drain
- Place for a minimum of eight weeks in a cool spot. They can be covered with polythene or peat but do not need dark. Ensure compost remains moist – not sodden
- After 8–10 weeks well-rooted bulbs can be stimulated with a little warmth. After a period of mild heat move the bowl to the warmer heated greenhouse, conservatory or living room. They must be kept in as light a position as possible otherwise lengthening stems reaching for light will weaken and collapse under their floral load

PEACH
(Prunus 'Peregrine'*)*

Walk onto the patio on a summer's morning and pick a fat juicy peach. What better way to pass a few minutes? This is the best cultivar: the only problem is coping with the juice likely to course its way down your chin.

type	Deciduous tree
flowers/fruit	Clear pink, mid-spring; cream-fleshed fruit, midsummer
foliage	Willow-like, narrow pointed
height	Dependent on the rootstock that it is grafted on to; for example 'St Julien A' supports a healthy but not overvigorous tree. Against wall 3–4m (10–12ft)
spread	3–4m (10–12ft)
soil	Ideally fertile, neutral or slightly acid and with open drainage. On chalky soils will need much extra humus and feeding to prevent lime-induced chlorosis (yellowed leaves)
site	Bush trees in warm, open site, fan-trained trees against walls facing the sun, not frosty spots
care	Plant first half of winter and stake firmly. Growth starts early. Leaf curl (fungus) can be prevented by covering fan trees with polythene from leaf fall until early to mid-spring, so preventing fungus spores landing. Prune in early spring by removing weak and badly positioned shoots and quarter cutting back stronger growths to encourage new growth. Unwanted side shoots can be pinched out in summer. Fruit is produced on last year's wood
propagation	You are unlikely to want more than one. Leave propagation to specialist nurseries
relatives	P. 'Duke of York', white-fleshed fruit, early; P. 'Barrington', yellow-fleshed, late. Ripe fruits of all these have excellent flavours

practical
project
1

RAISED BEDS AND
HOLLOW WALLS

PLANTS FOR RAISED BEDS

Nicotiana, scented forms
Pelargoniums, all types
Petunias, including trailing
types
Primroses
Verbenas
Wallflowers, best scented
strains

Raised beds and hollow walls suggest two different things: two extremes. Hollow walls are narrow, the gap between the two sides possibly only some 25–30cm (10–12in) wide; the walls tend to dominate. Wider than this is the raised bed proper, where the bed is more dominant than the walls.

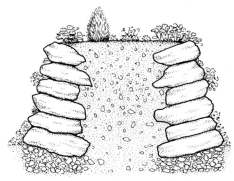

Cross-section of a raised bed

The benefits of both are not inconsiderable. The walls reinforce the form of the patio and add a suggestion of privacy to the enclosed space; they can enhance the microclimate created in the shelter of the patio. Raised above the ground, the bed or hollow wall spaces bring plants and flowers that much closer to the eye and to admiration; they also make their tending that much easier. Plants grow in the walls and others cascade down them. These constructions are easily made a feature full of lively interest all round the year and the structure itself should be pleasing to the eye.

If the patio is already bounded in part by a low wall, a second wall and ends can be built to make the bed, otherwise it is not very difficult to build the whole thing from scratch.

SITE AND DESIGN

The siting of beds is a vital part of the overall design and depends very much on the position of your patio and other garden features. An effective idea is to build a couple of beds leaving a gap between them to lead into the garden. Or, add an extra dimension by building beds that are obviously on different levels. Square beds are less visually appealing than rectangular ones. You may find an L-shaped one fits in.

Whatever their shape, beds should not be wider than it is possible to reach all parts comfortably by hand. This means 1–1.2m (3–4ft) wide if worked from one side and a maximum of 2–2.2m (6–7ft) if one can work from either side.

CONSTRUCTION CONSIDERATIONS

The walls can be built of stone, brick or wood: each of these offers diverse choices. The quickest building is achieved using railway sleepers. These are particularly apt against wood decking; a union of related materials but with one so much more massive, heavy and dark, rich textured. Three layers of railway sleeper laid down flat will give a wall of 38cm (15in) height. (Usual size for sleepers is approximately 2.45m x 20cm x 13cm [8ft x 8in x 5in])

Stone looks good and is a plant-friendly material. It is best to build courses of pieces roughly the same depth and bridge the gaps with the pieces on the next layer. A wall of three to four layers of thickish pieces making 30–45cm (12–18in) in height is normally about right. It can be higher for longer walls. Walls built of lots of narrow strips 2–5cm (1–2in) thick are not easy to maintain and offer too many crannies for slugs and snails.

Bricks, old or new, and either mortar-bonded or dry, can look in keeping. The mortar of each course adds about 7cm (3in) to the height (for cement mixes see p.27).

Remember to leave drainage holes in bonded walls and probably some random empty spaces where plants can be installed. Ensure that water seeping from these holes will not form puddles on the patio. If the patio butts up against the wall, the patio floor should slope away to dispose of wet. Alternatively, leave a narrow band of a few centimetres between bed and patio for a 30cm (12in) deep drain of rough hardcore topped with clean pleasing pebbles.

PLANTING

The structure itself must look right, but it is the plant life that will be the main visual fare to enjoy. Choose between a planting scheme that is more or less permanent, one that is seasonal or a compromise one which has permanent features backed up by ephemeral ones.

Permanent A permanent planting might consist of small shrubs underplanted with bulbs or perhaps a rock bed with a collection of alpines. Carefully thought out, both plans

will provide all year round interest. Once planted up the amount of upkeep is minimal.

Seasonal A succession of seasonal flowers and plants means planning and replacing plants season by season. If the patio is mainly used as an outdoor room in the summer, you can choose to concentrate floral displays for then. Traditional subjects are geraniums, lobelia and petunias. Colours available mean you can work to a definite scheme. Geraniums need not be flaming scarlet, there are fine whites and pale pinks; trailing kinds over the walls are very free flowering; you can pick kinds with attractive foliage and augment these with scented-leaved varieties – especially welcome on the patio.

Autumn and winter, when more tender things have gone, will be time for potted Michaelmas daisies to be plunged into position. Pots of *Nerine bowdenii* and other autumn bulbs are also drafted in for temporary duty. Ivies, *Euonymus fortunei* cultivars and winter-flowering heathers help defeat winter gloom

By spring a succession of bulbous plants will brighten the scene. These may be planted *in situ* or potted and plunged into their stations when in bloom.

A good compromise between permanent and ephemeral plants means choosing a number of basic shrubs and dwarf trees to give the whole a reliable skeleton staff, then adding colour with the seasons: spring bulbs; summer bedding plants; autumn bulbs and perhaps also potted pom-pom chrysanthemums and Michaelmas daisies.

SHRUBS FOR RAISED BEDS

Berberis thunbergii **'Atropurpurea Nana'**
Calluna vulgaris, in variety – acid soils
Convolvulus cneorum
Erica arborea alpina
E. carnea, in variety
E. × *darleyensis* types
Ericas, other kinds – acid soils
Hebe, in variety
Hydrangea macrophylla **'Mariesii Perfecta' ('Blue Wave')**
Hydrangeas, lacecap cultivars
Ilex crenata **'Mariesii'**
Juniperus × *media* **'Pfitzeriana'**
J. × *media* **'Pfitzeriana Aurea'**
Mahonia pinnata
M. × *wagneri* **'Moseri'**
Pinus mugo **'Mops',** and other good dwarfs
Rhododendrons, smaller kinds – acid soils
Roses, patio series
Spiraea **'Arguta'**
S. **'Goldflame'**

MICHAELMAS DAISIES
These are ideal for growing in pots and plunging into position when they come into bloom. Choose the mildew-resistant Aster amellus *cultivars such as:* 'King George', purple, 'Mauve Beauty', 'Violet Queen', 'Sonia', pink

plants

OF THE

month

2

▲ VIRIDIFLORA TULIP
(Tulipa 'Artist'*)*

A fine example of a Viridiflora tulip, the sturdiness of *T.* 'Artist' makes it particularly good for growing on the patio as it is easy to use in a variety of ways, as a pot plant, in a mixed container or for bedding.

type	Bulb
flowers	Large, round, a mixture of salmon, pink, purple, and green outside; inside salmon and green; mid- to late spring
foliage	Broad, grey-green
height	30–38cm (12–15in)
soil	Open textured, providing air and drainage
site	Sunny spot
care	Plant outside in autumn, with 12cm (5in) of soil over bulb tops. In containers plant early and have at least 5cm (2in) compost over noses
propagation	Lift and divide bulbs every third year, or annually if necessary, about five weeks after flowering
cultivars	Other Viridiflora tulips are taller. *T.* 'Spring Green' is an attractive

creamy white with bold green painting on the outer surfaces; *T.* 'Greenland' has neat flowers in green and pink

LILY-FLOWERED TULIP
(Tulipa 'White Triumphator'*)*

Lily-flowered tulips have a special elegance partly due to their flowers which are waisted with narrow pointed petals that tend to curve outwards. 'White Triumphator' is one of the stronger cultivars.

type	Bulb
flowers	White, firm-textured with petal tips neatly recurving; mid- to late spring
foliage	Broad, grey-green
height	65–70cm (26–28in)
soil	Open, quick-draining soil
site	Light, sunny spot in border or between shrubs
care	Remove dead flowers and any damaged leaves. Lift and divide bulbs every third year, or annually if need be, about five weeks after flowering
propagation	See care
relatives	Other lily-flowered tulips include very pointed, yellow *T.* 'Westpoint', red *T.* 'Aladdin' and pink *T.* 'China Pink', which is somewhat less pointed

◄ *TULIPA PRAESTANS*

This is one of the tulip species that can be planted and left for decades in the right spot. It needs sunshine and a well-drained soil that will become dryish in the summer. Given this the bulbs increase year by year and produce lots of flowers.

type	Bulb
flowers	Clean-cut flowers, one to five per stem, of oval petals a uniform glowing orange-red; early to mid-spring
foliage	Spreading grey-green leaves
height	10–40cm (4–16in)
spread	20–30cm (8–12in)
soil	Any well-drained
site	Open sunny spot, in a rock bed, front of border or in containers
care	Can be left for a decade in a suitable spot, but bulbs may be lifted and split up every three or so years. Do this about five weeks after flowering and replant straightaway

TULIP FESTIVAL

Want your own Tulip festival? The ones featured here are just a few of the many to choose from. For the patio, these could be good choices:

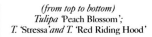

(from top to bottom)
Tulipa 'Peach Blossom';
T. 'Stressa'*and T.* 'Red Riding Hood'

plant	height	description
EARLY DOUBLES		
Short-stemmed paeony-like flowers very good for pots and other containers.		
T. 'Fringed Beauty'	*30cm (12in)*	*Wide flowers, fully-double, red with gold petal edges*
T. 'Monte Carlo'	*35cm (14in)*	*Very rich gold*
T. 'Peach Blossom'	*28cm (11in)*	*Rose pink*
KAUFMANNIANA HYBRIDS		
Dwarf, early and bright. For containers, rock beds, or front of borders.		
T. 'Heart's Delight'	*20cm (8in)*	*White and rich pink*
T. 'Showwinner'	*20cm (8in)*	*Brilliant scarlet*
T. 'Stressa'	*18cm (7in)*	*Gold with a red triangle on outer three petals*
GRIEGII HYBRIDS		
Similar to Kaufmannianas but usually a little later and often with attractive purple-striped leaves.		
T. 'Plaisir'	*15cm (6in)*	*Red with cream-lemon edges*
T. 'Red Riding Hood'	*8-12cm (20-30in)*	*Scarlet, with purple-striped leaves*
T. 'Toronto'	*25cm (10in)*	*Rich coral, several to a stem*
DARWIN HYBRIDS		
Huge leaves and massive flowers. Make a dramatic picture in large containers. In beds, bulbs can be left for several years – flowers will not be quite as huge after the first season but will still make a huge impact.		
T. 'Apeldoorn Elite'	*60cm (24in)*	*Scarlet and orange mix*
T. 'Daydream'	*60cm (24in)*	*Open lemon-gold but become suffused apricot*
T. 'Jewel of Spring'	*65cm (26in)*	*Cool primrose, pencil-line edge of red*
PARROTS AND FRINGED TULIPS		
Parrot tulips add a touch of the surreal and the fringed tulips impart unusual style.		
T. 'Flaming Parrot'	*60cm (24in)*	*Widespread, gold and red petals with lacerated edges*
T. 'Warbler'	*50cm (20in)*	*Neat rich golden flowers with much fringed petal edges*
SPECIES		
From very early spring till early summer, there are interesting species that are great for pots, mixed containers, rock beds, between heathers or at the front of borders.		
T. batalinii 'Bright Gem'	*12cm (5in)*	*Neat soft yellow warmed with some apricot*
T. chrysantha	*15cm (6in)*	*Neat pointed flowers red in bud, golden inside*
T. pulchella 'Violet Queen'	*10cm (4in)*	*Low leaves and globes of violet, very early*
T. urumiensis	*7cm (3in)*	*Flat rosettes of leaves, low golden flowers*

practical project 2

SCREES

PLANTS FOR SCREES

Acaena adscendens, pink
Acantholimon glumaceum, pink
A. ulicinum, pink
Anacyclus pyrethrum depressus, white
Anchusa caespitosa, blue
Androsace sarmentosa, pink
A. sempervivoides, pink
Aquilegia bertolonii, blue
A. flabellata nana, purple blue and light yellow
A. scopulorum, blue and white
Asperula suberosa, pale pink
Calandrinia umbellata, magenta
Carlina acaulis, cream
Celsia acaulis, yellow
Cichorium spinosum, blue
Convolvulus sabatius, mauve-blue
Edrianthus pumilio, lavender blue
Epilobium canum, grey leaves, scarlet
Erigeron aureus, see **Haplopappus brandegeei**
Eriogonum umbellatum, pale yellow

A scree garden adds an extra dimension to the patio. It may adjoin it or be seen from it and can make a contribution to the overall design of the garden as well as being an important environmental 'niche' for the alpine plants of the enthusiast. Once made, the scree will be the best spot for a range of small plants. Properly built, it will need very little attention and will remain interesting and pleasing through the year.

Normally, screes are sited to the side of a rock garden which may well suit your garden design; if it does not, you could choose to have a scree formally enclosed with a low wall, lower than those suggested for the more dressy patio-dominated raised beds (p.52).

A natural scree is formed by the continual erosion by weathering of mountain rock so that pieces tumble down the sloping mountainsides and accumulate as wide sweeps of small stones and rocks. In nature, these can sometimes be of surprisingly even-sized bits, but more usually there is a wide range of sizes. In a constructed scree bed the pieces are mainly 1–5cm (^{1}/$_2$–2in) in diameter and a more random appearance is achieved by incorporating a scatter of pieces several times this size and having a few quite sizable rocks apparently tumbled to their positions.

The shape could be roughly oblong with the sides defined by the edge of the rock garden, lawn or pathways. The path would look more in keeping if formed of York stone or imitation York stone, rather than anything more formal.

Sedum acre 'Aureum', Globularia meridionalis, Anchusa caespitosa and Silene acaulis make an attractive combination in this scree bed

SITING

Plants adapted to scree life will demand two factors before any others: drainage and light. Obviously in nature the scree is one of the most readily drained of all possible sites and it will be in full light. No good trying a scree under deep tree shade!

A sloping site is a huge natural bonus, with surface water draining away freely. On a flat site that is not all that well-drained, the scree may have to have a generous drainage channel, arranged from the site to lower ground or a more formal drain.

Procedure
■ Mark out the site with string or hosepipe.

■ Leave for a few days to reconsider the form and size. Normally the smallest worth attempting is 2–3m (yd) square.

■ Excavate soil to a depth of at least 30cm (12in): 45cm (18in) is recommended by some energetic and exacting practitioners.

■ Dig over the base of the excavation and

incorporate rough hardcore.

■ If needed arrange drainage away from the site possibly by a series of field drains laid at a slight slope to lower ground.

■ Add a 10–15cm (4–6in) layer of coarse hardcore.

■ Now add the main growing medium to bring the level up to that of the surrounding site or fractionally above this to allow for settlement. Use a mix of these approximate proportions by volume:

3 grit, gravel, chippings or crushed rock as single ingredient or a mixed lot
1 healthy loam, good garden soil or rotted grass turf
1 humus as leafmould or well matured compost

■ Allow to settle.

■ Add a scatter of larger rock pieces and a few random rocks.

■ Plant specimens. One or two dwarf trees or shrubs – especially evergreen ones – make useful focal points. Go for a natural effect by gathering a small community of plants in the shelter of each of the larger rocks.

MAINTENANCE

Scree plants may look tiny above ground but they develop root systems of extraordinary length and intricacy. However, after growing in pots, newly planted specimens will find the meagre fare of the scree very difficult and dry. Add a little more soil and humus around them in the gritty scree mix – tempering the wind to the scorn lamb – and then keep them watered generously for a much longer time than usual in the garden. They will take time to get exploring roots deep into the scree and become fully self-sufficient.

Keep the scree weed free – not difficult as the diet does not appeal to that many weeds – and apply the lightest possible dusting of general fertilizer at the winter's end, avoiding direct contact with plants. Alternatively, fertilizer can be applied with an extremely light dressing of sifted loam, humus and grit-dust in late autumn or early spring.

WATERING NOTE

■ *As the scree mix is so spartan and free draining it is a good idea to introduce a perforated pipe some 15–25cm (6–10in) below the final layer. Bring it to an unobtrusive spot at the surface of the scree so that a hose pipe can be attached and water introduced below in times of severe drought* ■

PLANTS FOR SCREES
Continued

Erodium reichardii, white and pink
Euryops acraeus, yellow
Frankenia alatamaha, pink
Globularia cordifolia, lavender-blue
Globularia repens, lavender-blue
Haplopappus brandegeei, yellow
Helichrysum bellioides, hairy mats, white
H. coralloides, silver and green erect shrublet
H. milfordiae, silvery foliage, red buds, white flowers
Leontopodium alpinum (edelweiss), white
Leptospermum humifusum, white
Minuartia stellata, white
Myosotis alpestris (alpine forget-me-not), blue
Nierembergia repens, white (moister spot than most)
Ononis cristata, full pink pea flowers
Onosma tauricum, silvery plant, yellow
Origanum calcaratum, pink and green
Raoulia, all tiny-leaved carpeters
Sedum, only introduce the choicer least rampant species
Sempervivum, in variety
Silene schafta, mauve-pink
Teucrium aroanium, lavender-blue
***Verbascum* 'Letitia',** shrublet, yellow
Zauschneria, see Epilobium canum

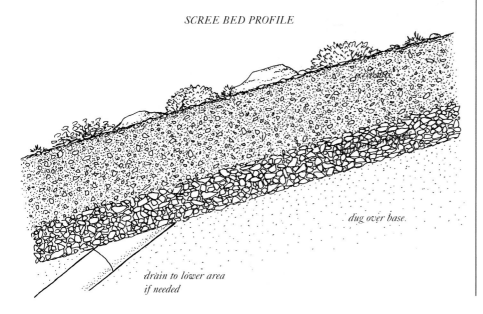

SCREE BED PROFILE

dug over base.

drain to lower area if needed

MAY

Surprisingly quickly, the first roses are out and early climbing kinds
are a picture. The garden and countryside is re-clothed; hedgerows and
trees are fresh in new green livery. All is exuberant growth and bloom
– the later daffodils and tulips are doing splendidly, many herbaceous
plants are growing rapidly, rock plants are still at their best, and
many shrubs are coming into their high season. Wisterias are likely to
be in full blossom, giving their annual spectacular.

More settled warm, dry weather means before the month is out, there
may even be rumours of the first mini-drought. In and by the patio,
shortage of water should not be serious, supplies are to hand and even
containers that threaten to dry out quickly are easily kept happy.
Water butts cleverly located close by, but hidden, come into their own;
the rainwater gathered from house and garage roof can be used
without any feeling of guilt about draining precious resources and it is
free of the lime and other chemicals that upset some plants.

On the patio, the less hardy plants can be given a chance.
Pelargoniums (geraniums) are growing and first flower trusses are
showing. Petunias, helichrysums, busy lizzies, lobelias and the
hundred and one annuals used in hanging baskets and other
containers are beginning to make useful growth and first flowers.
Enjoy the easy generous displays of annuals and half-hardy container
plants, but rely on other plants for a more heavyweight input to
decorative schemes. Topiary shrubs in splendid earthenware containers
or half tubs are looking fresh with new foliage. What about that shrub
in the form of a peacock in full display? And there are the large pots of
lilies now growing strongly, with one or two left under glass for
encouraging into bloom before the month's end.

Everything looks good.

tasks
FOR THE
month

FOLIAGE PLANTS

Alchemilla mollis
Aralia elata
Artemisia absinthium
Bamboo (Arundinaria)
Cornus alba 'Elegantissima'
Dicentra sp.
Eucalyptus gunnii
Euonymus fortunei cus.
Euphorbia characias
Gunnera sp.
Fern sp.
Liriope graminifolia
Macleaya cordata
Phormium tenax
Salix lanata
Sedum maximum
S. spectabile
Thalictrum various

CHECKLIST

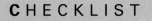

- Pruning shrubs
- Deadheading
- Foliage plants
- Planting out half-hardy plants
- Spraying

PRUNING SHRUBS

By the end of the spring many of the early shrubs have finished blooming and it is soon time to take the secateurs or shears to some (see also p.12). The idea is to cut away the wood that has just flowered to keep the shrubs within bounds and more importantly to encourage them to produce fresh new wood that will carry next season's blossom. Around the patio shrubs that are growing close to the house will look best groomed closely against the walls, which may be helping to support them and are certainly giving them the shelter and warmth that encourages the formation of ripe wood and lots of new flower buds.

The current flowering wood is cut back to a couple of buds: these will supply the new growth.

DEADHEADING

This has always seemed to me one of the dreariest of gardening jobs. Consequently it is not overdone in our garden, with the exception, however, of near the house and on the patio because here, with many plants, the more rigorously you cut away the dead flowers, the greater numbers of new ones you are going to enjoy. This is seen most clearly with bedding plants of all sorts, early roses may be persuaded to send further flurries of blossom and daffodils and tulips close to the house and in pots look tidier with their dead flowers removed.

So as the months become warmer and the days longer deadheading becomes part of the routine.

FOLIAGE PLANTS

This month some of the most worthy foliage plants begin to make their impact. Hostas make fine specimens in large pots and containers. Their bold sculpted forms are just what is needed on the patio; the strong lines and living colour contrasting well with the infrastructure (see opposite for suggested types). Purchase three distinct hostas, or – if you already have some in the garden – lift three clumps and plant them in three sizeable earthenware containers to make an impressive group from spring till the frosts.

Other foliage plants may be even more useful, especially the evergreens, such as the more interesting of ivies, which will still be on duty when the hostas are having their longish winter rest. In containers and close to the patio, it is important to have a selection of shrubs that are interesting throughout the year – variegated euonymus forms, hollies, camellias, brachyglottis and many others (see practical project p.128).

Many herbs have leaves that are good both to look at and to smell. It is useful to have some growing close to the house for the kitchen. (See opposite for suggestions.)

PLANTING OUT HALF-HARDY PLANTS

If not already done, most bedding plants should be hardened off by the end of the month (see p.49). Pelargoniums and the main lot of half-hardy plants should also be in their display stations. Hanging baskets sheltering under cool glass may be ready now or within a week or two.

SPRAYING

Being not all that fond of chemicals, I try to keep their

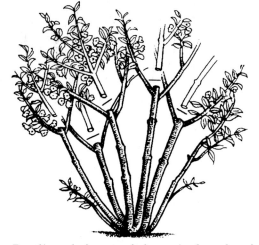

Forsythia, cut back to strong buds removing flowered wood

use to a minimum and make any spraying undertaken produce a maximum effect. It is best to spray early before trouble appears. Black-spotted, mildew-worn roses look tragic; use systemic fungicides before or as soon as you see trouble. One or two doses spring and early summer will have to suffice – and usually does.

HOSTAS

Most hostas have attractive leaves in all sizes and colours. Here are some favourites:

H. fortunei, large – plain mid-green

H. fortunei **'Albopicta'** – large, white-edged

H. fortunei **'Albopicta aurea'** – large, golden shades

H. **'Halcyon'** – smallish, blue-grey

H. sieboldiana – very large, blue-grey

H. sieboldiana var. *elegans* – extra large, bluer than *H. sieboldiana*

H. **'Zounds'** – good-sized, olive-yellow

Chives

IVIES (Hedera)

H. canariensis **'Gloire de Marengo'** – large dark leaves with cream edges

H. colchica **'Dentata Variegata'** – large polished leaves with varying amounts of creamy gold variegation

H. colchica **'Sulphur Heart'** – large leaves with yellow veining or irregular variegation confined to the centre

H. helix **'Anne Marie'** – quite wide grey-green leaves with cream edging

H. helix **'Buttercup'** – most leaves uniform bright yellow

H. helix **'Glacier'** – light green wide-leaved kind with pale yellow variegated edges

H. helix **'Goldheart'** – dark green irregular margins to rich gold centres

H. helix **'Harald'** – creamy white leaves with pale green patches

H. helix **'Sagittifolia Variegata'** – small leaves , very pointed and indented, well edged with cream

HERBS

Of the many herbs with good-looking and aromatic foliage you might like to try:

Chamomile *(Chamaemelum nobile)* – a low carpet of ferny green foliage, sometimes tried as a small lawn but better used less formally. The double form exchanges single yellow-centred white daisies for neat double blooms

Chives *(Allium schoenoprasum)* – neat with slender round upright leaves and rounded mauve flowerheads. Some clones are much neater than others

Dill and Fennel – filigree foliage, all light and feathery

Feverfew *(Tanacetum parthenium)* – light green foliage and lots of small daisy flowers. It is reputed to be good for migraines

Mints – many forms. Peppermint with purplish leaves, eau-de-Cologne mint is rather larger and refreshing. Pineapple mint has golden-variegated leaves

Wormwood *(Artemisia absinthium)* – a subshrub in demand for its silver-grey foliage

Feverfew

plants
OF THE
month
1

▼ YELLOW BANKSIAN ROSE
(Rosa banksiae 'Lutea'*)*

This is hardier than the type but is still best on a warm tall wall – it can grow up 10m (30ft) and as wide if given the chance. You can grow a clematis or other climbing plant with *Rosa banksiae* 'Lutea' as it only needs old, useless wood removing.

type	Climbing, deciduous thornless rose, a bit tender
flowers	Clustered, much doubled, yellow, not over 2.5cm (1in) across, unscented; late spring
foliage	Small, typical rose, pale green
height	10m (30ft)
spread	10m (30ft)
soil	Fertile, not sodden
site	Warm wall or sheltered, protected from excessive frost
care	Prune only awkward or damaged wood
relatives	*R. banksiae* is white, scented and

perhaps less hardy. *R. banksiae* 'Mermaid' is an old slow-growing climber with 12cm (5in) wide single primrose-yellow blooms over dark green foliage and thorny stems

COMMON PASSION FLOWER
(Passiflora caerulea) ▶

Passion flower features this month, not because it blooms now – it flowers summer and autumn – but because now could be a good time to plant a new specimen growing away strongly after the cool winter. This is the hardiest of the many fascinating passion flowers and grows easily and rapidly with tendrils clasping any aid to its extension. It is always a conversation starter, especially growing by the patio up the trellis on the wall or on a pergola.

type	More or less hardy, evergreen climber
flowers	White but flushed blue or pink and banded purple; many weeks through summer and autumn
foliage	Dark green leaves of five or more long leaflets
height	10m (30ft) if given the chance
spread	10m (30ft) if allowed along supports
soil	Fertile well-drained
site	Best in full sun by a wall or against supports that reflect warmth
care	Tidy up after winter by clipping worn pieces
propagation	By spring cuttings taken with a heel, 15cm (6in) long and kept in a propagating frame until rooted. Alternatively, it can be air layered
relatives	There is a fine ivory-white cultivar called *P. caerulea* 'Constance Elliot'. Other species are usually tender but *P. lutea* will probably survive in warmer areas and has flowers in a mix of white, creamy yellow and pink.

AIZOONIA SAXIFRAGE
(Saxifraga 'Tumbling Waters'*)*

'Tumbling Waters' is perhaps the most famous of all saxifrage cultivars, a quite extraordinary floral performer. It is a touch slow to start but an annual miracle in bloom and very well worth having in your garden. Watch out for neighbourly covetousness!

type	Evergreen, mat-forming perennial
flowers	Arching sprays of hundreds of crowded white flowers, quite buddleia-like. Flowering rosette then dies and others take over; mid-spring

type	Evergreen fern
flowers	None
foliage	Long tongue-shaped, straight-sided margin, tough, highly-polished, rich green, short-stemmed; makes a persistent clump
height	45–75cm (18–30in)
spread	45–75cm (18–30in)
soil	Not a gross feeder, will grow on poor soil and happy on lime
site	Not very fussy but best in shade or semi-shade and damp
care	Plant firmly but not burying crown in the ground. Keep checking it is moist until established
propagation	Divide clumps in early spring or early autumn
relatives	*A. scolopendrium* 'Crispum', a series of mutant forms producing upright rather flattened fronds with very attractive goffered edges which catch the light. *A. scolopendrium* 'Muricatum' has flat fronds with lightly goffered margins; it is a small, neat plant, often only a third, but possibly half as big as the type. Other cultivars have much crested or cut margins and lack a clean cut style; they look like mutants!

foliage	Tight, hard rosettes of narrow, grey-green leaves, encrusted with a white layer of lime
height	12cm (5in) but up to 50cm (20in) in bloom
spread	Plant to 18cm (7in) but arching flowerheads reach 50cm (20in)
soil	Gritty soil with lime
site	Miniature garden, rock bed, raised bed, sunny
care	Plant firmly then leave to establish. Slowish to grow
propagation	Careful separating of rosettes in early autumn
relatives	*S. callosa* with lime-encrusted rosettes and upright and arching sprays of white flowers, with small red spots.

HART'S TONGUE FERN

(Asplenium scolopendrium, syn. *Phyllitis scolopendrium)*

We do not always have to go to the ends of the world to find good garden plants; this fern is native to all countries of Europe. It is a great friend in the garden growing in many poorly lit spots both wet and quite dry on the poorest of soils.

M A Y

practical project 1

PLANTING HANGING
BASKETS

PLANT NUMBERS
A summer basket using
traditional plants will need:

BASKET SIZE	PLANT NUMBERS
20cm (8in)	up to 10 plants
25cm (10in)	up to 25 plants
30cm (12in)	up to 35 plants

Like gardening in earth-bound containers, hanging baskets have become hugely popular over the past few years, a result, perhaps, of shrinking garden sizes or of the complete absence of gardens. Usually baskets are arranged hanging from supports on the house walls, which is perfectly acceptable, but patios may also have partial or full scale pergolas, trellis work and other places from which to hang baskets. And, carefully sited, you will be able to see them from inside.

SIZES AND TYPES

The usual basket is made of metal wire covered with plastic. These are lightweight and entirely practical. Some baskets are entirely plastic and may or may not have built-in water reservoirs at the base. These can be effective and the slightly off-putting plastic effect is soon lost as the plants cover the whole thing. If none of the commercial types appeal, it is a comparatively simple thing to make your own baskets from wood.

The larger the better is really the main principle when buying. Baskets of 25cm (10in) diameter are hugely better than 20cm (8in) ones; the difference in volume is approximately double. There are baskets up to 40cm (16in) in diameter and even bigger. You can make a homemade basket any size and its square shape means the volume of compost it will hold is more than the conventional bowl-shaped ones.

The main constraint on size is the weight of the basket filled with compost and plants fully watered. Safety is a real concern: the support must be completely secure. With larger baskets, firm attachment is more easy to achieve when working from pergolas than when relying on angle wall supports held by rawl-plugged screws in brick or mortar.

CONSIDERATIONS

Lining
The basket must be lined. The old-fashioned method was to use a lining of moss; this is now rightly regarded as environmentally unfriendly – moss being an important constituent of vulnerable ecological sites. The main alternatives are plastic sheeting, coir fibre held by fine mesh plastic netting or purpose-made foam liners. These are ideal and can be cut into shape so they fit the semi-sphere and allow plants to be put in on the sides as well as at the top.

Compost
Good compost is important. The plants need a healthy soil with balanced nutrients readily available and a supply of slow-release fertilizer capsules. While huge numbers of successful baskets are filled with peat- or humus-based composts, these do have the drawback of being very difficult to get wet again if they should get over-dry. I prefer a soil-based mix with a generous input of humus.

Watering and water retention
The real success of the plants depends on a good water supply to the plants. Baskets with built-in reservoirs start with an advantage. Ordinary ones are made easier to water by installing a perforated funnel when filling them with compost. Nothing very elaborate is needed, the top of a plastic bottle will provide a reservoir into which the water can be poured, it will then permeate the whole basket (see also pp.48 and 74).

Moisture-retaining gels are available at good garden centres. These will significantly increase the water retention properties of a compost.

MAKING A SQUARE HANGING BASKET

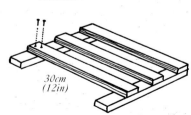

30cm (12in)

Use wood pieces 30×5×2.5cm. Treat with non-creosote preservative. Use brass or other non-rusting screws

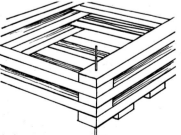

Drill narrow holes through corners of assembled pieces. Fix together with a long bolt or strong wire bent at the base and looped at the top

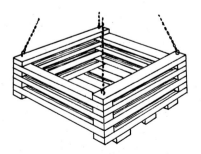

Arrange on a hanging chain. Remember the square basket takes a lot of compost and will be heavy. Do not exceed the size recommended, unless you have very secure fitments.

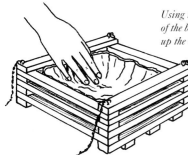

Using the chosen material line the bottom of the basket, taking the material part way up the sides (see text for alternatives)

Fill the basket one-third fill with compost (see recipes below)

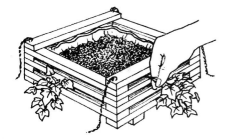

At this stage add a layer of trailing plants by pushing them through from the outside of the basket and firming them into the compost. Repeat this process with the next layer of trailing plants. Finally add the upright plants

PLANTS FOR SUMMER HANGING BASKETS

ANNUALS
Raise these from seed (F2 hybrids will give very good results).

Ageratums
Bidens ferulifolia
Brachycome iberidifolia
Busy lizzies *(Impatiens)*
Convolvulus tricolor
Gazanias
Geraniums *(Pelargonium)*
Lobelias
Marigolds *(Tagetes)*
Pansies
Petunias, especially trailing kinds
Stocks
Tropaeolum majus (semi-trailing nasturtiums)
Verbenas
Zinnias

PERENNIALS
Begonias, large-flowered
Begonia semperflorens, for trailing
Argyranthemum (Chrysanthemum) frutescens 'Jamaica Primrose'
Fuchsias
Geraniums *(Pelargonium)*
Helichrysums
Ivies *(Hedera),* in variety
Osteospermums

COMPOSTS

Ready-made hanging basket composts are offered by many garden centres. If making your own, base it on these proportions by volume:
- *1 healthy loam*
- *1 humus (peat, mature compost, leafmould)*
- *1 grit*

To this can be added a general fertilizer which could be close to the John Innes base formula, parts by weight:
- *2 hoof and horn, 2–3mm (¹/₈in) particle size*
- *2 superphosphate of lime*
- *1 sulphate of potash*

To this add ground limestone:
For every 36 litres, (8 galls/64 pt) add 100g (4oz) John Innes-base fertilizer and 20g (³/₄ oz) ground chalk.

PLANTS

Choose a balance of plant types to give the greatest possible impact. Bushy, upright and, of course, trailing kinds, all need a place. The best effect is usually obtained from a crowded planting.

MAINTENANCE

■ Ensure regular watering. Each day in normal weather. Even on rainy days your baskets may have missed out: do check. The ideal is a trickle irrigation scheme which supplies water for a period each day direct to each basket. Otherwise it means using a hose, watering can or a long-shanked pump specially-made for delivering water to the baskets hanging above head level.
■ If the compost nutrients needs boosting, a liquid feed can be given once a week. This is not excessive – just think how much growth depends on the tiny amount of compost.

PLANTS FOR WINTER HANGING BASKETS

Box *(Buxus)*
Euonymus fortunei, varieties
Heathers
Ivies *(Hedera)*
Lonicera nitida 'Baggesen's Gold', shaped specimens
Narcissus, small, such as *N.* 'Tête à Tête', *N.* 'Jumblie'
Primulas, including polyanthus and primroses
Winter-flowering pansies

plants
OF THE
month
2

HERBS BY THE PATIO

The patio seems a natural place for herbs, the most domestic of plants. They are ideal gathered close to the kitchen door where they are easy to harvest for culinary or medical uses and can be enjoyed for their fragrance as well. They can be a very decorative feature, especially if tackled boldly. Those featured are just a few of the many available. A list of other good herbs is in the margin.

▼ SAGE
(Salvia officinalis)

With its persistent foliage, sage should provide you with fresh leaves for picking all year, however, they can also be dried successfully.

type	Evergreen sub-shrubby perennial
flowers	Stems of small, hooded pale purple flowers; midsummer
foliage	Grey, rough-textured, oval leaves
height	60cm (24in)
spread	1m (3ft)
soil	Any provided it is not sodden
site	Open sunny spot
care	Easy, but benefits from having sprawling bits cut back. Best replaced regularly

propagation	Easily raised from seed or cuttings taken midsummer
relatives	*S. officinalis* 'Purpurascens' is very pleasing with pale purple foliage and also has a cream-variegated form. *S. officinalis* 'Icterina' has grey leaves irregularly, but boldly, edged and dotted cream

▲ CULINARY THYME
(Thymus vulgaris)

Thyme's aromatic leaves are best used fresh but if you prefer to prune off the flowering tops the leaves on these can be stripped and dried.

type	Small evergreen sub-shrub
flowers	Rather insignificant pale lilac summer flowers – often trimmed off
foliage	Very aromatic small mid-green leaves
height	15–20cm (6–8in)
spread	20–30cm (8–12in)
soil	Not fussy if not waterlogged
site	Open sunny
care	Clip as needed. Replace every few seasons
propagation	Easy from seed, by layers or early summer cuttings
relatives	*T. serpyllum* is the very useful low-spreading species with many named forms, all good for growing between paving stones and lots of other places. *T.* × *citriodorus* is very lemony-scented and cultivars of this hybrid such as 'Golden Queen' and 'Silver Queen', which make attractive mounds of neat foliage, are well worth growing, even if less lemony

MINT
(Mentha spicata)

Mint is famous for its leaves, used in mint sauce, salads or with cooking potatoes or peas.

type	Rampant herbaceous perennial
flowers	Rounded lilac heads
foliage	Serrated oval leaves
height	60cm (24in) if allowed
spread	Can be invasive
soil	Not fussy
site	Open or shade
care	The main consideration is confining the energetic rootstock: sunken bottomless buckets, slates or polythene barriers may help
relatives	Bowles mint, *M.* × *villosa* 'Alopecuroides', is a superior, rounded-leaved kind. *M.* × *piperita* is the purplish-leaved peppermint, and *M.suaveolens* 'Variegata' is the pleasing pineapple mint

CHIVES
(Allium schoenoprasum)

This is one of the neater allium species with erect, narrow round leaves forming clumps.

type	Clump-forming bulb
flowers	Decorative thrift-like heads of pinky-mauve; late spring to summer
foliage	Hollow, narrow, upright blue-green leaves
height	15cm (6in)
spread	20cm (8in)
soil	Not fussy
site	Open
care	Easy plant
propagation	Division of clumps, best in early spring or early autumn
relatives	There are various clones of chives available, the smaller and more compact ones are much to be preferred to the rather coarse taller ones. *A. tuberosum*, Chinese chives, is white-flowered and with a half-strength garlic flavour

▼ GOLDEN LEMON BALM
(Melissa officinalis 'Aurea'*)*

The leaves of lemon balm are used in cold drinks and in both sweet and savoury recipes. They also make a herb tea.

type	Herbaceous perennial
flowers	Tiny and insignificant
foliage	Handsome, golden and green leaves as a mat but then flowering stems reach up
height	60cm (24in)
spread	40cm (16in)
soil	Not fussy
site	Open or partial shade
care	Easy plant; some shade will help prevent sun-scorch of leaves
propagation	Division
relatives	The type is a robust mid-green plant. No important other species

OTHER HERBS

Angelica **(Angelica archangelica)**
Aniseed **(Pimpinella anisum)**
Basil **(Ocimum basilicum)**
Bay **(Laurus nobilis)**
Bergamot **(Monarda didyma)**
Borage **(Borago officinalis)**
Caraway **(Carum carvi)**
Chamomile **(Chamaemelum nobile)**
Chervil **(Anthriscus cerefolium)**
Coriander **(Coriandrum sativum)**
Cotton lavender **(Santolina chamaecyparissus)**
Cumin **(Cuminum cyminum)**
Dill **(Anethum graveolens)**
Fennel **(Foeniculum vulgare)**
Feverfew **(Tanacetum parthenium)**
French tarragon **(Artemisia dracunculus)**
Ginger **(Zingiber officinale)**
Horseradish **(Armoracia rusticana)**
Hyssop **(Hyssopus officinalis)**
Lavender **(Lavendula angustifolia)**
Lemon verbena **(Aloysia triphylla)**
Lovage **(Levisticum officinale)**
Marigold **(Calendula officinalis)**
Orris **(Iris** 'Florentina'**)**
Parsley **(Petroselinum crispum)**
Rosemary **(Rosmarinus officinalis)**
Rue **(Ruta graveolens)**
Sorrel **(Rumex acetosa)**
Southernwood **(Artemisia abrotanum)**
Sweet Cicely **(Myrrhis odorata)**
Winter savory **(Satureja montana)**
Woodruff **(Asperula odorata)**
Wormwood **(Artemisia absinthium)**

practical
project
2

DESIGNING KNOT
GARDENS

KNOT GARDENS TO VIEW
A list of knot gardens to visit can
be found on page 142.

The long history of knot gardens associated with larger houses and palaces has been brought very much to life in recent years with the restoration or excavations and replanting of quite a number to the original plans and the planting of entirely new ones following traditional methods.

Knot gardens were almost invariably sited close to the house, their symmetry and formality being in keeping with the building. Many are best viewed from first floor windows. They were frequently areas for walking – a little gentle outdoor exercise and fresh air before dealing with the next roast ox! Despite their rather grand ancestry, it is perfectly feasible to create your own knot garden whether your dwelling is in the stately or 'unstately' class.

DESIGN

Choose a site that is easily visible from the patio, it can be close by or at a distance, depending on the shape of your garden. A very small knot could be incorporated into one corner of the patio or could border one side of it.

Size depends on the site and personal choice. Even two or three square metres (yards) could support a small knot. The basic idea is to produce a permanent pattern from miniature hedges in an unending scrolled or geometrical form. The interstices are planted up with varying – usually much smaller – plants for seasonal colour and interest. The whole seems almost closer to embroidery than gardening, but done well the effect can be peaceful and pleasing.

PATHS AND HEDGES

Getting the hedge work right is vital, but almost as important are the paths; the design is very heavily committed by these two features. The usual manner is to have permanent paths of washed pea gravel or chippings. Grass is allowed although, what with mowing and edging, requires more work than you may want to invest. If gravel or similar material is chosen the next decision will be whether the paths are to be curbed with brick, Victorian rope or other manufactured edging stones. Obviously such an undertaking will add very considerably to the cost.

PLANTS FOR THE PERMANENT HEDGES

Box is still very much the preferred plant for miniature hedges. The slow-growing form of common box, *Buxus sempervirens* 'Suffruticosa', has been used for centuries and is still probably the best plant, albeit one that takes a while to grow large enough to start serious trimming. There is also a variegated form, with leaf edges narrowly margined in cream.

For a quicker result, the impatient might fancy *Lonicera nitida*, the rapid-growing, small-leaved evergreen, popular for interior hedges. It is certainly worth considering if you are happy to be trimming the hedges frequently. With a powered tool it is a pleasure rather than a hardship. The golden-leaved form *L. nitida* 'Baggesen's Gold', while still fast-growing, is less rampant than the standard green.

A very attractive, easy and low-growing alternative is provided by heathers. A very pleasing pattern can be made using *Erica carnea* forms, variety being introduced by combining rich green ones with golden ones, such as 'Westwood Yellow'. A couple of light trimmings will keep all tidy for the twelve month. Or you might consider very good dwarf clones of lavender. The fragrance would be a welcome addition.

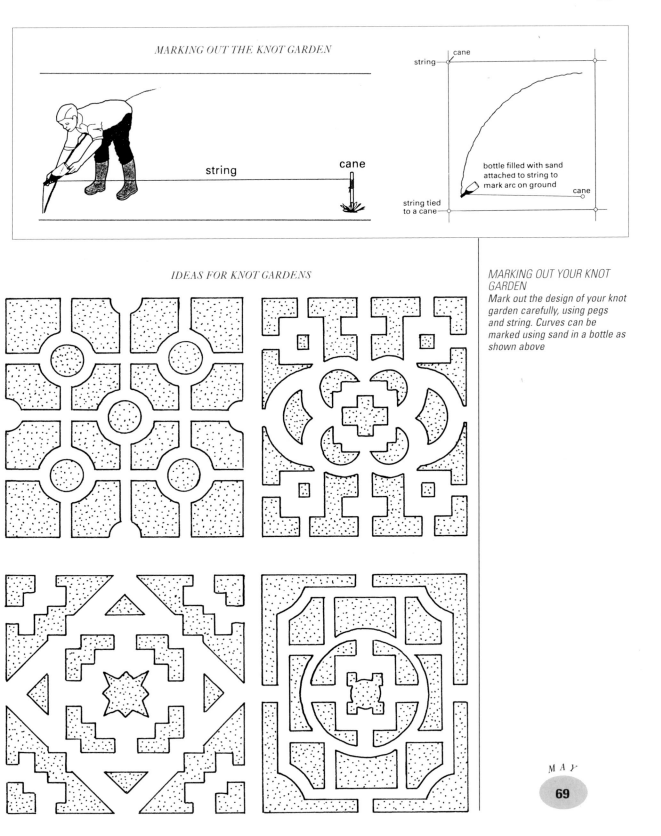

MARKING OUT THE KNOT GARDEN

string

cane

cane

string

bottle filled with sand attached to string to mark arc on ground

cane

string tied to a cane

IDEAS FOR KNOT GARDENS

MARKING OUT YOUR KNOT GARDEN

Mark out the design of your knot garden carefully, using pegs and string. Curves can be marked using sand in a bottle as shown above

M A Y

practical project 2

DESIGNING KNOT GARDENS

(continued)

PLANTING

Box and other hedging plants need to be planted closely, 20–25cm (8–10in) intervals being the maximum. This means that a lot of plants are needed to form the hedge. If you are not in a rush, it makes good economic sense to buy a few plants and to propagate these intensively to give the required number before attempting the whole layout. A two stage plan will allow reasonable progress: fast growing outer hedges could be installed as stage one, the inner ones being added when enough further plants are available. Obviously it will take some while for this second lot to catch up with the initial planting but at least you will have staked a claim on the piece of ground and will be on a learning curve.

Heathers, lonicera and lavender are all easy to propagate from cuttings. Box is a little slower.

Propagating box

- Choose a time in late summer to undertake this task.

- Fill 7.5cm (3in) square pots with compost of equal parts peat and perlite or fine coarse washed/grit but leaving a 1cm ($\frac{1}{2}$in) gap at the top. Water the pots.

- Using a sharp knife, collect cuttings about 7–9cm (3–3$\frac{1}{2}$in) long.

- Remove leaves from the bottom third of each cutting.

- Dip cut ends into hormone rooting powder and knock off the surplus.

- Insert cuttings in pots – a minimum of 5, maximum of 9 – ensuring all leaf-stripped lengths are in compost.

- Place pots in a tray or propagator sunk into peat or a similar material.

- Lightly spray with fungicide and enclose with a rigid plastic top.

- Place in a light spot but not in direct sunshine. A corner in the open near a wall might be suitable.

- Only remove the lid when condensation seems to have dried off – this is the signal for watering. Replace immediately.

- Only open the propagator vents when the cuttings have started to grow and make fresh leaves.

- From then on give high potash fertilizer feeds at monthly intervals.

- Pot up individually when each cutting has got two or more new leaves and roots are active.

- When established, plant out in a nursery row and grow on for a season or two before planting in their permanent positions.

Lonicera cuttings can be lined out in a shady spot and kept moist. Use pieces not less than 15cm (6in) long, with at least half in the soil. Heather and lavender can be treated in a similar manner to box: heather cuttings need only be about 5cm (2in) long.

EPHEMERAL PLANTING

Inside the hedges the choice of plants is without limit. You may want uniform colours and restrict the selection to bedding plants such as pansies, mignonette, tagetes or bulbs such as scillas and hyacinths. You may choose to have a permanent planting of small herbaceous plants, a less labour-intensive plan than the more frequently adopted seasonal bedding schemes. Permanent arrangements could combine the lowest-growing heathers, small hebes and thymes with some neater silver- and grey-leaved plants such as dianthus. Seasonal plans could include winter- and spring-flowering pansies, dwarf kaufmanniana tulips, primroses and polyanthus followed by busy lizzies, petunias and the neater pelargoniums for summer. For autumn try dwarf potted michaelmas daisies, colchicums and crocuses; and in winter ivies, variegated euonymus and pansies. Collections of low-growing herbs would be an interesting possibility. The idea of herbs and sweet smelling plants close to the house is as traditional as the knot garden.

MAINTENANCE

The success of the knot garden depends on constant attention to detail. This means repeated trimming and ensuring that the foliage cover is as even as possible from ground level upwards. Pegging down branches to maintain healthy green lower levels may be necessary.

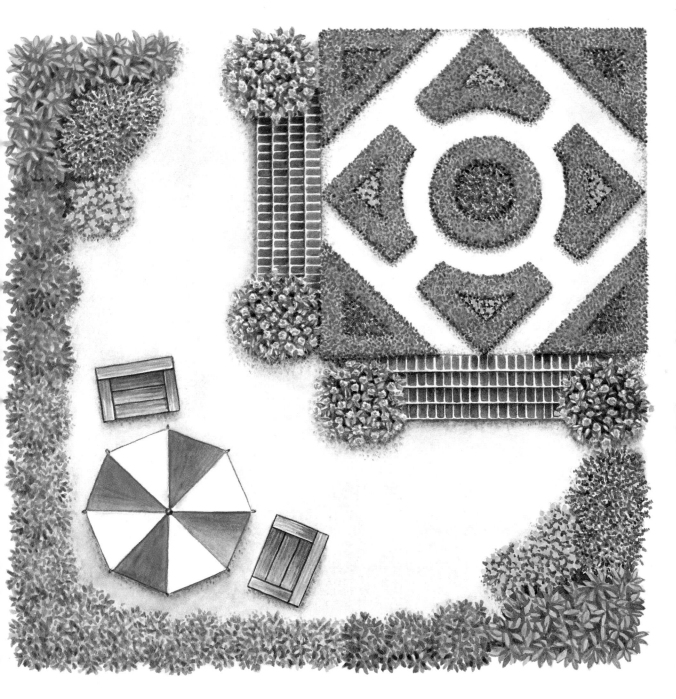

*Steps lead up from the patio to this stunning
knot garden feature*

JUNE

With the longest days of the year, the garden, the patio in particular, is coming into its own. Now herbaceous perennials and annuals, in beds and containers, are all energetic activity. Pergolas are densely covered with foliage and flower. On the patio, pots of lilies are in full bloom, marguerites (Argyranthemum frutescens) *produce more of their white ox-eye flowers daily and coloured forms, such as* A. 'Jamaica Primrose', *brighten the scene. What a good idea it was to take cuttings early last autumn!*

In the little pool by the patio, miniature water lilies show buds and tadpoles are turning into small adult frogs – a tricky time for them, when predators may be queuing for a tasty breakfast. Fledgling birds are beginning to feel their way in the wide world; pairs of blackbirds are starting second broods – gluttons for punishment.

Genista lydia *spills a treasury of gold over a low wall. Further away,* Spiraea × vanhouttei *and others enwreath every twig with white blossom. The scents of roses and cut grass invade the air.*

Between the patio stones, the prostrate thymes are creeping and they too add their perfume to the scene especially when trodden on; they do not seem to mind, provided they are not constantly crushed. Their first flowers appear now and the ground-hugging Anacyclus depressus *opens dark red buds to display startling white daisy flowers to the sun, closing them again if it turns very dull.*

It is no bad time. And, here on the patio someone has placed a glass of cool white wine. It must be mine. Cheers!

tasks

FOR THE

month

PLANTS FOR CRADLES
All those plants suggested for hanging baskets (p67) are suitable for cradles. Cradles can take larger plants so you can have more of the Argyranthemum (Chrysanthemum) frutescens 'Jamaica Primrose'-type plants that become bush-like. Osteospermums also come into their own with the extra rootrun. You may decide to give the cradle early backbone with shrubs – perhaps a golden privet or two.

CHECKLIST

- Cradles
- Water saving
- Box and mini-hedges
- Mulching
- Tending lilies

CRADLES

Cradles perform a similar function to hanging baskets but they are usually fixed closer to the ground, which makes watering easier, and they can be very much larger, so allowing many times the amount of compost and a larger number of plants — and larger ones. They are ideal for gardeners with little or no real garden space. One, two, three or more in a courtyard can bring about a transformation.

Make sure that the metal cradle is well lined with punctured polythene, perforated plastic sheeting or spongy sheeting as sold for hanging baskets. (Moss is not recommended as it has to be ripped out of the wild, thus spoiling natural habitats.)

Drainage is important but more still is the healthy soil/compost structure. The mix should allow plenty of air and humus. A good combination is healthy loam, coarse grade peat or similar humus, and grit in equal amounts by volume, together with a sprinkle of general fertilizer and appropriate doses of slow-release fertilizer capsules. (See margin for planting suggestions.)

WATER SAVING

All growing success depends on adequate water supply. Try to locate a waterbutt — or two — nearby. If you are worried about appearance it is easy enough to erect a trellis and train some climbers up it to disguise the water butt. In containers and raised beds, arrange ingress points for watering so that precious water is not just scattered over the surface and a significant proportion lost to evaporation (see tasks pp.48, and 86).

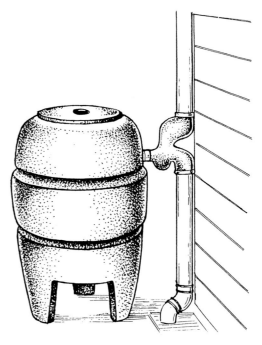

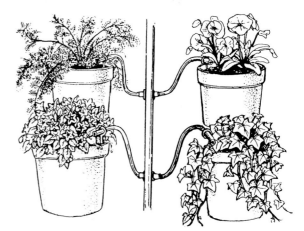

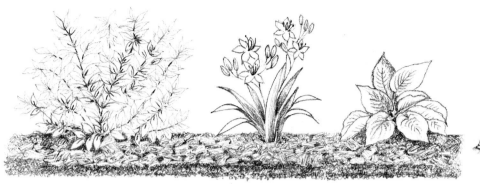

Mulch of shredded bark 7–10cm (3–4in) deep

BOX AND MINI-HEDGES

Trim box as you wish. Small hedges are best cut lightly but fairly frequently — two, three or four times a year rather than just an annual event. This applies even more to hedges of *Lonicera nitida* or *Berberis thunbergii* and other strong growers; their quicker growth requires extra clipping to maintain a crisp kept appearance.

MULCHING

Mulches act in several beneficial ways: they suppress weed growth; they help conserve water; they improve overall appearance; and some mulch materials help feed the plants.

Suitable materials

■ *Compost*. Well rotted, this has an attractive dark crumbly appearance. It is a feeding help and friendly towards soil organisms.

■ *Shredded bark*. This is good for stopping weed growth and is a good insulation material that allows water through and helps retain it. It is also attractive.

■ *Gravel, rock chippings*.

They can make a very pleasing contrasting effect around plants. They insulate roots from heat, allow all water to pass into soil easily and then help retain it.

TENDING LILIES

Lilies will be growing strongly now. They can stand drought better than many plants, but the energetic roots and transpiring leaves will be making big demands on the soil water. Soak pots in large buckets of water; thoroughly soak containers. Where there may be a threat of lily beetle check plants for both the scarlet-red adults and the larvae. After flowering move the lilies away from the patio but keep them watered. It is a good idea to sink the pots into the soil or plant a garden site with a whole group.

HANGING BASKETS
This is likely to be the first full month of your summer hanging baskets. The plants are still growing very strongly. Ensure they receive no checks due to inadequate watering.

LIFTING BULBS
Make a resolution to lift and divide any overcrowded or misplaced bulbs either this month or next. See p.87.

LILY BEETLE

These fast working pests can strip a lily of leaves. In Britain they are more or less restricted to the south, especially the Home counties. Keep an eye out for them and pick off any larvae or adults you find. Place a sheet of paper below before starting, beetles that fall to the ground can be difficult to find despite their scarlet dress. Larvae look dirty – like bird droppings.

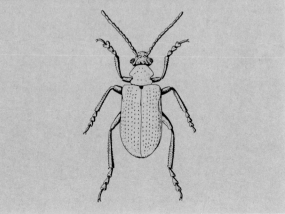

plants
OF THE
month

HOSTA
(Hosta sieboldiana)

This is a leading foliage plant which comes into leaf in spring and dies down in mid-autumn with the first frosts. Its impressive leaves can be up to 30cm (12in) long and 20cm (8in) wide. It can be used for ground cover or if preferred it is ideal for growing in ample pots on the patio.

type	Herbaceous perennial
flowers	Sprays of very pale lilac, tubular flowers somewhat hanging; early summer
foliage	Huge, heart-shaped, deep veined, ribbed and rich steely blue-green
height	45–75cm (18–30in)
spread	75cm (30in)
soil	Not fussy, but best in healthy soil
site	In sun or shade: excessive sun may accentuate the green rather than the blue of the leaves. Containers, allowing plenty of room for extensive root system, or beds. Likes moisture
care	Easy
propagation	Split clumps end of winter
relatives	*H.* 'Gilt Edge' has large, rich green leaves with broad yellow margins (see also p.61)

HIDCOTE LAVENDER
(Lavandula angustifolia 'Hidcote'*)*

This compact lavender is ideal used as a spot bush near the patio or used to make a low hedge. It is certainly easier to keep trimmed neat and low than the larger types which often seem to want to fall apart leaving gaping centres.

type	Evergreen shrub
flowers	Dark purple-lavender, mid- and late summer
foliage	Silvery-grey, aromatic, narrow straight-sided
height	60cm (24in)
spread	60–75cm (24–30in)
soil	Fertile, open-textured, happy in lime
site	Sunny, well-drained
care	Prune lightly in spring to keep tidy or trimmed as a dwarf hedge
propagation	Seed is readily produced and will germinate freely to give similar, but varied, offspring. To make a uniform hedge take semi-ripe cuttings from a good specimen in summer
relatives	*L. angustifolia* 'Munstead', similar with rather paler flowers. *L. dentata* is a larger, French lavender producing flower spikes with showy purple bracts. Ht. 1m (3ft)

PATIO LILIES
(Lilium 'Orange Pixie'*)*

'Orange Pixie' is one of a series of genetic dwarfs that are especially good in pots or containers on the patio. All are sturdy and wind resistant. Once you have bulbs you should be able to propagate stock and have surpluses for planting out in beds near the house.

type	Bulb

flowers	Upward-facing, bowl-shaped, bright orange with a scatter of small dark spots towards the centre; early summer
foliage	Bright rich green, polished, strap-shaped, neatly alternately displayed, not quite horizontal
height	30–38cm (12–15in)
soil	Not fussy, but best open textured with humus
site	Containers, beds
care	Plant in autumn or spring with 10cm (4in) compost or soil over noses
propagation	Either split clump of bulbs, or use scales to produce series of new young bulbs
relatives	There is now a wide choice of Pixie hybrids (see p.13), and other suitable lilies are listed on p.43.

PATIO ROSE

(Rosa 'Bright Smile')

Patio roses are halfway between miniature and floribunda types and are notable for their ease of culture. They are also very floriferous and produce long lasting displays. *R.* 'Bright Smile' is particularly bushy and neat.

type	Deciduous rose
flowers	Lots of clear yellow slender buds opening in time to show stamens; in succession through summer
foliage	Well furnished with polished leaves
height	60cm (24in)
spread	75cm (30in)
soil	Well worked, healthy
site	Border or bed
care	Trim in winter
relatives	Wide range of colours and flower shapes: *R.* 'Esther's Baby', rose-pink semi-double stars in graceful sprays, 40cm (16in) high bush. *R.* 'Peek-A-Boo', lots of pinky apricot flowers on compact rounded bushes 45cm (18in) high and wide. *R.* 'Anna Ford', lots of semi-double orange-red flowers, spreading bush 45cm (18in) high

Patio roses are available in a variety of colours. They produce displays over a long period and are easy to care for

practical project

BUILDING PERGOLAS AND TRELLIS

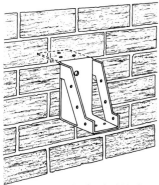

A galvanized joist hanger with the top part set into the wall. The beam is screwed securely into the cradle

Pergolas and trellis are useful additions to the patio. Positioned over the patio, a pergola provides a false ceiling, allowing you to have a growing canopy overhead; at the same time it makes the patio seem larger and more private – a room-like enclave. A covered patio is a house extension at a cut price, and may prove a very useful way of linking different structures, such as the garage and the house, and of covering up inadequate or poor building design. Pergolas are also often used as covered walkways; the patio can be the start of such a structure. They can also be sited so as to block out an unfortunate view.

Wooden trellis, in various patterns, can be used to create walls that will support lots of different kinds of plants, but especially climbers, such as those from the huge and diverse *Clematis* genus. Trellis walls or screens, not being solid, are all the more enticing; they break up space and can seem to enlarge it. Used to half mask an area, they add a little mystery, which can be a very important element in the design of the patio.

● PERGOLAS

Design factors
There are three main parts to a pergola: the uprights, the cross-beams and the runners linking one arch to the next. The main structure will give support for climbing plants and this can be augmented by tautly-fixed wires or trellis. Pergolas can be any shape or size you wish, covering the whole patio or just a part of it. You may like to take the following into consideration when planning your pergola:

■ Except in very large scale plans, and some country properties, broad heavy pillars of brick or stone will look out of proportion with the horizontals above: for preference use timber or metal for the uprights.

■ The height of the horizontal beams should be above the level of ground floor windows, but do not make it easy for an intruder to gain access to house through upper windows.

■ Usually, the simpler the design, the more effective the result: ornamentation comes from the plants.

■ The structure needs to support its own weight and those of any plants growing up it; it needs to be able to resist the force of winds. A few heavyweight uprights will pro-

vide the same amount of strength as a greater number of slender ones, which however may be more aesthetically pleasing.

■ Materials that echo those of the house, or other garden structures, are most appropriate; use the best that you can afford.

■ Take care in the construction, the structure must be very secure, otherwise it may become dangerous.

Materials
■ *Uprights:* rustic poles are a possibility, but can look skimpy, especially near the house. Metal scaffolding is sensible: it can be painted black, dark green, or whatever colour looks right, and the ends can be closed with wooden dowels to facilitate fixing to the cross-beams. Plain wooden posts in the 7.5 x 7.5cm (3 x 3in) range are also suitable.

■ *Cross-beams:* these can be made from 22 x 5cm (9 x 2in) lengths of wood of the type used for floor joists.

■ *Fixings:* a wall plate is ideal for fixing the cross-beams to the house wall. This is a piece of wood running the length of the pergola and firmly fixed to the wall with substantial screws into rawlplugs. Better still, use expanding bolts which are like expanding rawlplugs but made of metal and very powerful. Galvanized joist hangers, which are like boxes cut diagonally (see illustration) are an alternative to a wall plate. Firmly secured to the wall, these provide sockets into which the beams can be dropped and then fastened with screws.

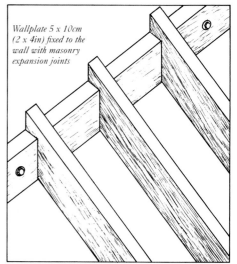

Wallplate 5 x 10cm (2 x 4in) fixed to the wall with masonry expansion joints

■ *Metal housing units:* these are essential for protecting the part of the wooden uprights that go into the soil, ensuring they have a longer life.

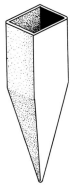

■ *Cement* for making-good house masonry and, if needed, for concrete housing for uprights in place of metal units.

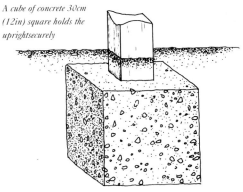

A cube of concrete 30cm (12in) square holds the upright securely

■ *Timber preservative,* or buy ready treated timber.

■ *Assorted screws and nails.*

Before buying any materials, make a scaled plan of the pergola to enable you to calculate how many cross-beams and uprights you will need. *(Continued on page 80.)*

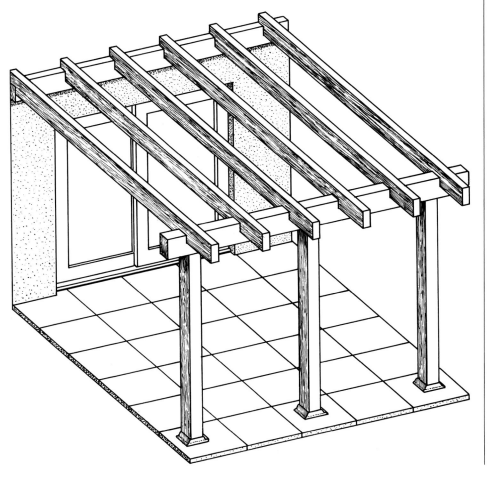

PLANTS FOR PERGOLAS

ROSES
The climbers including:
R. **'Blush Rambler'**, light pink, Ht. 3m (10ft)
R. × *centifolia* **'Muscosa'**, old pink moss, Ht. 1.2m (4ft)
R. **'Climbing Ena Harkness'**, scarlet-crimson, Ht. 2.5m (8ft)
R. **'Climbing Mrs Sam McGredy'**, salmon, Ht. 3m (10ft)
R. **'Easlea's Golden'**, butter-yellow, Ht. 3m (10ft)
R. **'Golden Showers'**, golden-yellow, Ht. 2.5m (8ft)
R. **'Mme Pierre Oger'**, pink, Ht. 1.2m (4ft)
R. **'Reine des Violettes'**, violet purple, Ht. 2m (6ft)

HONEYSUCKLES (*Lonicera*)
These are fragrant unless stated otherwise
L. × *brownii* **'Dropmore Scarlet'**, scarlet-red, Ht. 4m (12ft)
L. etrusca, pale yellow, but darkening and flushing red with age, Ht. 4m (12ft)
L. japonica **'Aureo-reticulata'** has rounded green leaves dominated by golden veining and suffusions, and white flowers becoming yellow, Ht. 10m (30ft)
L. periclymenum **'Graham Thomas'**, white becoming yellow, Ht. 7m (22ft)
L. p. **'Serotina'** (late Dutch honeysuckle), dark purple and pink, Ht. 7m (22ft)
L. sempervirens (coral honeysuckle), pink-red and orange, not scented, Ht. 4m (12ft)
L. × *tellmanniana*, yellow and orange, not scented, Ht. 5m (15ft)

(continued overleaf)

practical project

BUILDING PERGOLAS AND TRELLIS

(continued)

PLANTS FOR PERGOLAS (continued)

VINES (*Vitis*)
If you want to harvest grapes for eating or wine-making, choose the earliest ripening kinds, the latest normally feasible is **'Chasselas d'Or'**, which ripens in mid-autumn
***V.* 'Brant'** – strong growing with good foliage, nondescript fruit, Ht. 8m (24ft)
***V. vinifera* 'Purpurea'** – attractively shaped purple leaves, with a light downy appearance, and tight bunches of dark grapes, Ht. 7m (22ft)
V. coignetiae – a very strong climber, with very large, roughly heart-shaped leaves, up to 20cm (8in) across, good autumn colour, Ht. capable of growing over 18m (50ft)

Clematis – species such as **C. montana** will cover wide stretches of pergolas quickly. The large-flowered hybrids can be grown through other climbers and provide summer and autumn bloom

TRELLIS AND SCREENS

Trellis may be used on one or more sides of the patio to provide privacy as well as attractive plant supports. Viewing the garden from the patio is made more interesting and gives the illusion of much greater space if the eye is interrupted by one or more partial screens made of trellis. Ready-made units, which may fit the bill, are available in most garden centres, but otherwise, for a small screen, a firm framework of 5 x 5cm (2 x 2in) timbering can be erected and the trellis fixed to this. A more substantial screen will need stronger posts: suitable sizes being about 7.5–10cm sq (3–4in sq). While initially the open screen may not be under huge strains, as climbing plants grow up it, the stresses will increase in proportion to the size of the plants, their weight plus their effect as a sail in the wind.

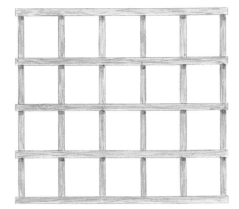

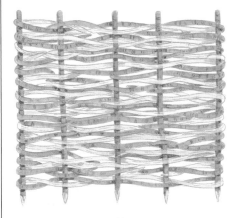

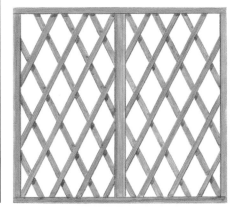

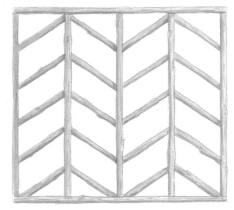

DECEIVING THE EYE

A walkway from the patio into the garden can be made a little more impressive by exaggerating the perspective effect. This is done by gradually reducing the width of the walkway as it retreats into the distance. Cleverly constructed screening fixed against walls can also be used to create a false perspective.

PLANTING

There may be a temptation to use a large variety of different climbers. You can, but it is better to aim at a bold planting, using fewer varieties for greater effect. Consider using just one plant of huge-leaved vine, *Vitis coignetiae*, allowing it to run over much of the structure, or planting several specimens of the same climbing rose, giving a sense of unity that is missing from a mixture. The planting can then be supplemented with a series of clematis. Or you could choose a wisteria. Wisterias are often thought of as taking next to forever to grow and flower; this is not necessarily so. Several kinds bloom as very small specimens and, once planted, grow apace.

Remember winter. If only deciduous plants are used, the structures could look gaunt after leaf fall. Coloured ivies trained on uprights would go a long way to avoiding this. (See margin for planting suggestions.)

MAINTENANCE

- *Check structures thoroughly at least each autumn to ensure that no supports are becoming rotten or loose. Particularly check any work done against the house wall*
- *Treat woodwork periodically with wood preservative to lengthen its life and to freshen its colouring*
- *Prune roses and other climbers in early winter or when appropriate*

MORE CLIMBERS FOR PERGOLAS AND SUPPORTS

Ivies – See p.55 for suggestions

Jasmine – *Jasminum nudiflorum* can be tied in to grow up and along the supports for yellow winter flowers. *J. officinale* produces sweet scented white flowers through summer and autumn

Passion flowers – *Passiflora coerulea* is hardy with white flowers, probably flushed blue and pink. Several others are also very effective

Solanum crispum '**Glasnevin**' is usually evergreen with lots of purple potato-flowers with gold centres

Wisterias – All are spectacular in bloom. *W. floribunda* '**Macrobotrys**' can have racemes as long as 1–1.2m (3–4ft) of lilac and purple flowers. There are forms that produce blossom as very young plants

plants

OF THE

month

2

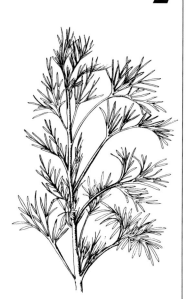

WORMWOOD

(Artemisia absinthium 'Lambrook Silver')

Wormwood may sound medieval and bitter but this plant is one of the very best of the 'silvers' – those plants that light up the garden through much of the year and that have foliage which looks good through long periods of sun and drought.

type	Evergreen, bushy, woody-based perennial
flowers	Insignificant, grey flowerheads; not prolific
foliage	Filigree silver leaves, finely divided and sparkling
height	70–80cm (28–32in)
spread	60–80cm (24–32in)
planting	Firmly; early autumn or early spring
soil	Not too rich, open-structured, free-draining
site	Best in an open sunny spot
care	Can be pruned back to within 15–18cm (5–6in) of base at end of winter. Cut away flowering heads. Give some frost protection in very cold areas
propagation	Easiest by layering low stems in summer, detaching and planting out rooted pieces in spring
relatives	*Artemisia ludoviciana* var. *albula* with undivided, long, pointed leaves shines silvery white with upright stems. It is bigger, at 1.2m (4ft) high by 60cm (24in) wide, and has narrow plumes of grey-white flowerheads in summer

MOUNT ATLAS DAISY

(Anacyclus pyrethrum var. *depressus)*

One of the huge daisy family (*Compositae*) but distinctive with its ground-hugging habit, this is a plant that can bear close inspection and is useful as it blooms in early summer when the main flush of small alpine-type plants have finished their displays.

type	Prostrate perennial with a central tap root
flowers	Red buds open to bold flat white daisies with central yellow discs. Young flowers close in poor light
foliage	Attractive much-divided, ferny leaves in a rosette and from the stems, growing from a central point. Dark matt-green
height	5cm (2in)
spread	30cm (12in)
planting	Early spring, using young plants and

trying to avoid damage to tap root

soil	Better in poor gritty soil than fed with riches. Dislikes constant wet and so needs first-class drainage
site	Open sunny spot, trough garden, rock garden or bed, scree, front of a heather bed
care	Lives for a few years; sow seed in late summer or take cuttings in spring to ensure continuity of possession
propagation	See care
relatives	No better close relatives but other smaller daisies include *Anthemis cinerea*, with silvery cut leaves, and *A. montana*, which makes a cushion of woolly foliage

DECORATIVE ONION

(Allium christophii, syn. *A. albopilosum)*

Onions may sound all culinary utility but there is in fact a wealth of beautiful species and varieties in a genus perhaps 1,000 strong. The species featured is one of the most splendid: distinct, opulent and easy, it is splendid for dried arrangements as well as on duty in the garden.

type	Bulb
flowers	Spectacular spheres, up to 30cm (12in) across, of 50 or more narrow-petalled stars of shining purple-violet: the petals look almost metallic and lie flat to emphasize the sphere shape. Early summer
foliage	Semi-erect, narrow, grey-green leaves that droop at tips and may begin to die off by flowering time
height	30–40cm (12–16in)
spread	20–30cm (8–12in)
planting	Newly purchased bulbs early autumn, home-grown ones in summer
soil	Unfussy but will not tolerate constant

sodden conditions

site Open spot with surrounding plants to mask dying foliage

care Easy. The ripening and ripe seedheads are highly decorative and will be so *in situ* certainly till late summer. For use in dried decorations cut and dry fresh flowering stems, or the equally impressive seeding heads

propagation Huge quantities of seed are produced and germinate freely outside but the tiny bulbs take perhaps four years to reach flowering size. Bulbs split steadily rather than frenetically

relatives *A. aflatunense* has purple flowers in 10cm- (4in-) wide, tight balls in summer. Height 75cm (30in). *A. karataviense* blooms in late spring with broad, arching, purple-grey-green leaves and round heads, 15cm (6in) across, of pale mauve-pink flowers. Height 20cm (8in)

DWARF RHODODENDRON
(*Rhododendron* 'Elizabeth'*)*

Stately homes and parks are not the only places for rhododendrons, there are some rel-atively modest-sized kinds that are hugely prolific in bloom and neat when flowering is over. Of course, they do not like lime.

type Evergreen shrub

flowers Lots of rich scarlet-red trumpets; late spring into early summer

foliage Oblong, rounded, tough rich green

Rhododendrons make attractive subjects for patio containers

leaves making a handsome rounded, neat, well furnished shrub

height Eventually 1.5m (5ft)

spread Eventually 1.5m (5ft)

planting Early autumn or late spring

soil Acid soil, preferably rich in leaf-mould or peaty humus

site In sun or half shade

care Remove dead flowerheads. Mulch to keep shallow rooting system moist

propagation By layers or cuttings in early summer

relatives *R. yakushimanum,* neat, 1m (3ft) high by 1.5m (5ft) wide shrub with oval leaves, silvery when young but dark green when mature. Pink buds open to near white trumpets in late spring. All hybrids of this species are tidy and useful in smaller gardens

JAPANESE SHIELD FERN
(*Dryopteris erythrosora*)

Dryopteris is a huge family of ferns, found worldwide. This species, also called 'autumn fern', is one of the neatest and easiest of garden plants. It is large enough to be very effective but not too large for smaller gardens.

type Fern

flowers None

foliage Horizontally spreading triangular fronds, neatly divided and polished. Young fronds are coppery pink, after some months this turns to bright green. Foliage can last through winter but in very severe winters may be deciduous

height 30–45cm (12–18in)

spread 30–45cm (12–18in)

planting Early spring or early autumn. Do not plant the crown deeply, it should remain at the same soil level as it was in the pot

soil Moist, humus-rich, open-structured

site Preferably in half shade

care Not fussy. Do not allow this shallow-rooted plant to dry out. Keep weed free

propagation Divide in early spring or, second best, in early autumn

relatives Some of the smaller mutants of the male fern, *D. filix-mas,* are tidy and attractive, more or less evergreen plants. *D. affinis* 'Cristata The King' is a splendid plant with nearly parallel-sided fronds, edged and terminated with crests (much divided ends). The fronds are erect but then arching outwards. Height 50–90cm (20–36in)

JULY

High summer: containers are overflowing with colour, patio plants are in carnival dress and bees work overtime carrying their loads of nectar and pollen. Gardeners keep almost as busy, but relish the long hours of sunshine and the colour all around. The silver-leaved plants and the collection of Mediterranean-types are looking their best. Insects are doing quite well too, hopefully kept in check by the birds; smaller predators also graze on the aphids. Moths come by evening and night to visit evening primroses, honeysuckle, night-scented stock and the flowering stems of nicotiana. Encourage them: there are not the numbers and varieties there were a few decades ago.

There is just a hint of hurry and bustle: the grass needs an extra cut and the borders could do with a tidy as the holiday season approaches. The patio looks neat enough, although watering requirements need to be arranged before any absences. Sometimes you may wonder whether it is worth the effort. Of course it is!

Make the most of your patio while the good weather lasts. At odd times, pause, rest; take a well deserved break in the gardening rounds. Invite friends around to help clear a bottle or two. This really is the way to garden. The honeysuckle, roses and clematis are in a loving tangle on the pergola; all around is gorgeous flower and scent.

Not all is just for show. Against the wall the espalier peach trees hold swelling fruits for all the family. Along the pergola, vines provide welcome shade and are promising lots of juicy bunches to eat and to convert into 'Chateau Dun Romin'. It is going to be a vintage year.

tasks
FOR THE
month

CHECKLIST

- ☑ Automatic/semi-automatic watering
- ☑ Mediterranean plantings
- ☑ Tying-in and training climbers
- ☑ Lifting bulbs

AUTOMATIC/SEMI-AUTOMATIC WATERING

There are several automatic watering systems, falling into two basic types: sprays and seepage. Before deciding what system you wish to use it is worth noting that with the increasing use of water and subsequent shortages, water companies are empowered to demand that gardeners using garden sprays install water meters. The perforated pipes used in seepage systems are also counted as sprays. An average garden sprinkler uses the same amount in one hour as an average household of four uses for all other purposes over two days!

Sprays

A spray fitting fixed onto a hose that joins the mains at an outside tap is the easiest system to install. A non-return valve at the point that water moves from the interior domestic supply to the garden is now a required fitting. The sprayer is moved around after the area treated appears wet. Using the sprayer in the evening ensures there is considerably less water lost to evaporation than using it during the middle of the day. Some good is done by soaking the foliage with water but it is the amount that reaches the roots that is the real measure of success. In the summer the sprayer is not going to win top marks for efficiency. Remember: if you are metered every drop has to be paid for.

Seepage

Seepage waterers come in various forms. Some are simply pipes with holes. The more efficient of these are those with two pipes — an interior pipe with holes at 1m (3ft) intervals that allows water out into an outer pipe with holes at approximately 30cm (12in) intervals. The pressure levels are more uniform along the pipe than in a single pipe where the holes nearest the mains supply are under greater pressure than those at the pipe's end.

Easily the most efficient of the seepage systems are those consisting of a supply pipe fitted to the mains supply with feeder lines leading off it at right angles and with adjustable nozzles or valves at intervals along these lines. A nozzle is opened to allow a drip of water against the plant, container or tray you wish to irrigate. The flow can be adjusted using fingers — tools will soon strip threads. These systems are installed relatively easily and the main pipes are soon disguised by a covering of mulch. They are

particularly useful for large containers — half an hour twice a week will suffice in normal times; in very dry hot weather the frequency can be increased. Alternatively, a number of small pots can be grouped and stood on capillary matting within a shallow plastic or metal tray. The matting and tray can be obscured by small grade gravel and a nozzle allowed to water the capillary matting and thence the pots.

Efficiency of the watering will depend on water pressures, placement of the sprayers/nozzles and the cleanliness of the system. A thorough filter system will help to keep nozzles from jamming up, but make regular checks. A timing device to allow watering to take place at regular fixed intervals is certainly a huge help, although you need to keep an eye on the outflow to avoid making unnecessary extra contributions to water company profits.

MEDITERRANEAN PLANTINGS

As summers seem to be getting dryer and water more scarce, it makes sense to choose some plants that can cope more easily with long dry periods. The Mediterranean climate, which has little frost, mild winters, early springs and long summers, supports a range of flora. Use of Mediterranean flora will bring

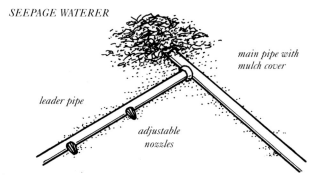

SEEPAGE WATERER

main pipe with mulch cover

leader pipe

adjustable nozzles

A Mediterranean bed of drought-resistant plants can be enhanced by the seasonal addition of a few potted specimens

to mind the patios of this warmer part of the world, no bad thing, and should be looking its best just when we are using the patio more for our leisure time and social activities. First are the bulbous plants that get their work done well before the hot dry days of summer. Then there are the perennials that conserve their water with foliage that is covered with silky hairs to restrict transpiration – giving the appearance of silvered leaves. To be most successful, Mediterranean plantings need to reflect the habitat typical of the Mediterranean – long sweeps of gravel, with stones of different sizes, echoing a shoreline or a river bank are effective; a few substantial weather-smoothed boulders will add considerably to the appearance. Formal beds can work just as well if that is what you prefer.

The site needs to be well-drained, with properly prepared weed-free soil, and it needs to be as warm and sunny as can be managed. (Suitable plants are given in the margin.)

TYING-IN AND TRAINING CLIMBERS

The climbers will be growing strongly now and new growth may need tucking into trelliswork or tying to supports such as pergolas. It is as well to try to keep a useful proportion of new growth, and thus flowers, low on the plant. This may mean bending down some branches. Exuberant growers against a wall can be curbed by gentle pruning now; keep a constant check on any *Chaenomeles* to keep them within bounds and to encourage plenty of twiggy growth, which equals lots of new flowering wood, close to the wall. Established wisterias

will be ready for a fairly hard pruning in late summer. At present restrict yourself to nipping out any obviously redundant flailing growths.

LIFTING BULBS

Spring bulbs that need lifting – overcrowded and misplaced clumps – really should be dealt with this month if they were not tackled last. Daffodils, tulips, crocuses, scillas, muscaris and almost all early bloomers can be carefully lifted, shaken free of soil, split up and replanted, either in fresh sites or back into redug and newly fed soils – some compost and a sprinkle of potash with a little general fertilizer will suffice. Replanting immediately is recommended: bulbs left in store are easily forgotten, can be mixed up, are vulnerable to rodents and can lose vitality if over-dried.

MEDITERRANEAN-TYPE PLANTS

BULBS
Allium, species
Crocus, species
Cyclamen coum
C. hederifolium
Fritillaria, species
Iris reticulata, types
I. juno types
Muscari, species
Narcissus, dwarf hybrids
N. jonquilla
N. rupicola
Snowdrops (*Galanthus*)
Sternbergia lutea
Tulip species

HERBACEOUS PLANTS
Anacyclus depressus
Convolvulus sabatius
Eryngium, smaller types
Euphorbia, various
Gypsophila repens
Helleborus foetidus
Limonium latifolium
Saponaria ocymoides
Sedum, various
Sempervivum, various
Waldsteinia ternata

SHRUBS
Artemisia, various
***Brachyglottis* 'Sunshine' (*Senecio*)**
Cistus, various
Convolvulus cneorum
Euonymus fortunei, cultivars
Rock rose (*Helianthemum*), various

plants

OF THE

month

1

▼ CASCADE GERANIUMS/ PELARGONIUMS
(Pelargonium)

Geraniums crowd the top of the queue for places on and around the patio. They do not all have to be blazing scarlets, the whites and pale pinks can play a role as well as the scented-leaved kinds. The very attractive cascade kinds are widely grown in Europe, especially in Switzerland and Austria.

type	Half-hardy perennial
flowers	Huge quantities of single flowers in many colours, including scarlet, rose-pink, lilac-pink, white, pink with white eye; early summer until the frosts
foliage	Rich green, divided into lobes
height	From top trails to 60cm (24in)
spread	38cm (15in)
soil	Good John Innes-type potting compost, gritty
site	Windowboxes, hanging baskets, tubs, down walls
care	Treat as other geraniums. Not fussy
propagation	Summer cuttings, kept frost-free over winter
relatives	Ivy-leaved trailing geraniums can also be very effective with rather succulent foliage and flowers often semi-double such as 'Belladonna', light pink; 'Luna', white with light pink flush; 'Bernado', a full red

ORIENTAL LILY
(Lilium 'Sans Souci'*)*

It is difficult to think of anything which can rival the opulence of the Oriental lily hybrids. In size, colour and textures they are breath-

taking, and as you approach them you cannot escape their wonderful fragrance. *L.* 'Sans Souci' and the other orientals respond well to container cultivation and will earn you a reputation of gardening wizard!

type	Bulb
flowers	Large, outward-facing, wide and nearly flat, white, suffused pink, deeper in the centre and with crimson spots; margins and tips white; richly perfumed; summer flowering
foliage	Dark green, alternately arranged, 15cm (6in) long
height	1m (3ft)
soil	Open-structured, neutral or acid
site	Containers or flower bed; light or sunny
care	Plant autumn or spring. In containers use ericaceous compost and cover with 10cm (4in) depth over the tops. Keep pots out of severe frost and not sodden over winter. Repot in fresh compost when they die down
propagation	By division of bulbs or, more intensively, by raising new bulbs from broken scales inserted into equal mix of grit and peat
relatives	A good persistent kind, *L.* 'Black Beauty' has more recurved flowers of very dark crimson and pink. Stems can carry from 10–150 flowers! It is tolerant of some lime. Once planted it can be left alone. Other lilies are listed on pp.13 and 49

BUSY LIZZIE
(Impatiens 'Picotee Swirl Mixed'*)*

Hybrid busy lizzies represent a major success in plant breeding. A relatively minor plant has been groomed to perform a major role in container and bedding work. Colours can satisfy those with the most flamboyant taste but there are cooler shades for more restrained planting schemes.

type	Half-hardy F1 hybrid annuals
flowers	Picotee shaded colours including whites, pale, dark and rose pinks, apple blossom and apricot orange. Bloom covers plants through summer until frosts
foliage	Bright green, but lost under the flowers
height	20–25cm (8–10in)
spread	30cm (12in)

soil	Fertile, well-balanced compost with slow-release fertilizer
site	Does well in shade or full sun
care	Sow late winter; they will germinate in under a month at around 23°C (73°F)
propagation	By seed, though cuttings will root
relatives	*I.* Starbright is a bicolour series, violets, oranges, reds and pinks. Many other fine strains are available

▶ TRAILING PETUNIAS
(Surfinia and Cascade petunias)

For hanging baskets, window boxes and similar sites these petunias are ideal. The Surfinia range are usually sold as small plants by colour; the Cascade strain are more likely raised from seed and can be raised by colour or mixed. There is no difference in habit.

type	Half-hardy annual
flowers	Round, wide open trumpets; various colours, but most in whites, soft pinks, mauves, purples and bicolours; through summer till autumn frosts
foliage	Oval, light green, soft-textured
height	20cm (8in), but perhaps 1m (3ft) or more hanging
spread	30cm (12in)
soil	Fertile, good quality compost with slow-release fertilizer
site	Hanging baskets, windowboxes, in raised beds to fall down the sides
care	Sow at the end of winter, prick-out seedlings and grow on to plant up into baskets/containers, under cover until danger of frost is over. Or, buy 'plugs' (small starter plants) and grow on or, later, larger plants
propagation	See care

JULY

practical project 1

CONSIDERING FURNITURE AND FEATURES

Furnishings are a major factor in establishing the atmosphere of the patio. A few loungers tell a different story to traditional upright heavy teak items or ornate cast metal tables and chairs.

ASSESSING NEEDS

Consider the following:

Amount How many are there in the family? How many will want to be sitting on the patio? Are there children? Can walls serve as perching places?

Permanent sites Any heavy or obviously immovable seats really should give a reasonable view of the garden. Give thought to sunshine, shade and shelter.

Movability Do you want to move pieces of furniture to other parts of the garden on occasion? This is easier done with lighter weight plastic artifacts than heavy teak.

Storage Some items may be meant to stay in position around the year, others are brought out for the good weather. Where will you store them?

Stability Any table should be steady and large enough to be practical when eating outside. Will you be entertaining? Is there a barbecue?

Sun and shade Some shade from the sun may be provided by overhead structures and plant growth. Even so, you may want to have a sunshade either as part of a table or as a free-standing item. Even when not in use it can look summery.

Containers Your patio may already be boasting permanent containers, half-barrels, trough gardens or classical urns overflowing with flowering plants. Leave space to walk around.

MATERIALS

Teak Well designed teak furniture can be left outdoors all year. It is expensive, but not when one thinks of its lifespan. While often formal and traditional in design, more modern styles are available; some of the circular tables look modern and yet are unlikely to date.

Cane Strong cane furniture suggests planter's bungalows in far-flung exotic spots, along with warmth and sunshine. Quality is variable but well-made rattan items can be extremely durable.

Metal-framed chair with padded seat cushion

Fully reclining lounger with adjustable leg-rest and sunshade

Well-strutted table for a rock-steady footing in lightweight metal

Plastic The range of plastic garden furniture is now very wide and not all is 'cheap and nasty'. It is best to avoid the occasional way-out colour, but dark greens and white are always acceptable. In terms of comfort, some plastic seats are way ahead of the good-looking and expensive wooden or metal offerings. They have the very great advantage of being designed to stack.

LUXURIES

Once the main items – chairs and tables – are chosen, then perhaps you can indulge yourself and pick a lounger or two. These vary from a deck-chair to a well-engineered teak 'steamer'. Here again consider movability: look for an item that is easily brought out for the 'open lounging season'.

Other luxuries you might like to consider are sundials or small pieces of statuary: both available from larger garden centres and elsewhere. These can do much to enhance the patio or the view from it.

STORAGE

At the end of the season the items going into storage need cleaning and storing in a dry place where they will not be in the way, perhaps in the summer house, garden shed or conservatory. Any cloth or foam parts should be stored safely out of the way of naughty rodents.

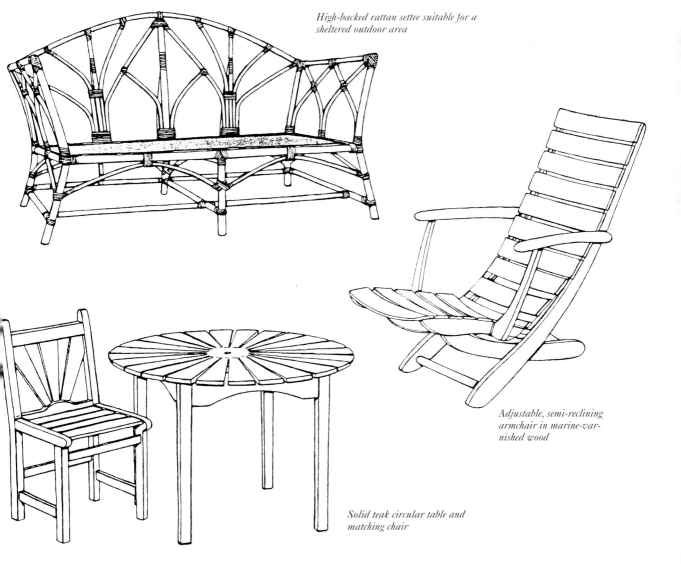

High-backed rattan settee suitable for a sheltered outdoor area

Adjustable, semi-reclining armchair in marine-varnished wood

Solid teak circular table and matching chair

plants
OF THE
month
2

Creeping thyme is just one of the many pretty plants which you can plant in the gaps between the slabs on your patio. The other plants which have been used here include sedum, dianthus, armeria and sisyrinchium

CABBAGE PALM
(Cordyline australis 'Atropurpurea')

The Australian cordylines are often grown in large earthenware pots and taken under cover for the winter. Exceptionally good sculptural plants, they can normally be thought of as perfectly hardy.

type	Evergreen foliage shrub, hardy in all but coldest areas
foliage	Narrow, pointed rich burgundy-red leaves, very evenly spaced as a globe from the growing point
flowers	Of little importance, terminal sprays of white summer flowers on long established plants
height	1m (3ft) in five years, 10m (30ft) in 30–50 years
soil	Provided it is well-drained, cordyline is tolerant of most soils
site	Warm, open spot
care	May need winter protection in exceptionally hard weather; wrap in fleece, sacking or sheeting
relatives	Various clones of *C. australis* are on offer; the standard is green-leaved

CREEPING THYME
(Thymus serpyllum coccineus)

This is the creeping form of thyme that is so useful in troughs, or to grow in the gaps between stones of paths. Small rooted pieces planted in the spring will quickly make headway and withstand treading well.

type	Prostrate, evergreen sub-shrub
flowers	Dark red, in crowded whorls sitting on the foliage; midsummer
foliage	Small, oval, dark purple-green, aromatic
height	1cm (1/2in)
spread	60cm (24in) or more
soil	Best in gritty soil that does not get too dry
site	Sunny spots, between paving, in trough gardens, in rock beds or at the edge of raised beds
care	Trim off dead flowers if you can, repropagate frequently using rooted pieces
relatives	*T. serpyllum* has many colour forms – whites, pinks and reds, some with very tiny leaves such as 'Minimus' and 'Minor'

PURPLE VINE
(Vitis vinifera 'Purpurea')

All vines are have attractive foliage but this neat one is particularly good, with leaves that are tough, compact and very colourful. It grows strongly but not quite so rampantly as some of the more vigorous vine grapes.

type	Hardy deciduous climber with tendrils
foliage	Neat decorative three- or five-lobed, purple-red leaves, which are covered with white fluff in their infancy
flowers	Small, pale green flowers in summer
fruit	Tight bunches of small, dark purple fruits, with 'bloom', persist till leaf-fall
height	To 7m (23ft)
spread	To 7m (23ft)
soil	Happy in most except very wet ones
site	Wall, pergola or to grow up a tree. Best in a light position
care	Prune to keep within bounds
propagation	Take cuttings of ripe wood about 30cm (12in) long. Insert two thirds into open ground after leaf-fall. Roots best in gritty soil
relatives	All vines look attractive in growth – though they start rather later into leaf than most other climbers. Of the vine grapes, the green 'Chasselas d'Or' is the latest ripening one that is practical for picking. For wine-making try: 'Muller-Thugau' green; 'Seyval

Blanc' (Seyve Villard 5276) prolific, green; 'Brant' very good autumn colour, indifferent grapes; 'Madeleine Angevine' quite early good green

Some are less fragrant. There are dwarf strains only 25–30cm (10–12in) high, such as *N.* 'Breakthrough Mixed' that start blooming early

TOBACCO PLANT

(Nicotiana alata 'Lime Green'*)*

Stroll in your personal garden of Eden after a hard day's work and be greeted by a rising cloud of evening perfume from the flowers of tobacco plant. Some plants will persist for two or three seasons. The fragrance of the flowers is especially noticeable in the evenings.

type	Half-hardy, short-lived herbaceous perennial, usually grown as an annual
foliage	Pale green, wide, flat oval, to 18cm (7in) long
flowers	Racemes of long-tubed, star-shaped lime-green flowers; late summer and autumn
height	60–75cm (24–30in)
spread	45–60cm (18–24in)
soil	Well-worked and fertile
site	Sunny, open spots
care	Sow seed in late winter or early spring, prick-out seedlings, grow on and plant out after frosts
propagation	See care
relatives	Various colour forms are available, some noticeably two-toned with the back of the petals much paler.

SOLANUM

(Solanum crispum 'Glasnevin'*)*

A relative of the potato, this is a hardy scrambling climbing shrub that can be very useful in sun or shade to fill an awkward corner or mask an undistinguished shed.

type	Evergreen/semi-evergreen, woody, clambering climber
flowers	Clustered, starry, purple, with prominent central pointing spike of gathered orange-gold stamens, like potato blossom; midsummer–late autumn
foliage	Oval, rich green
height	6m (20ft)
soil	Well-worked, open-textured
site	Sunny spot where it can find support, perhaps a warm, sheltered wall
care	Tie branches to supports, cut out weak and overcrowding growth in spring
propagation	Layer low branches or air layer. Summer cuttings
relatives	This is the best form

practical
project
2

MAKING A
BARBECUE AREA

Eating outside gives an extra dimension to our living pattern. Cooking outside adds fun to the ritual, despite smoke in our eyes and carbon in the eatables! Meat-eaters note: the carnivores among us might think that barbecues are of little interest to vegetarians, in fact, cooking outside can be fun for all.

The first decision is whether to have a barbecue or not, if the enfranchised voting goes in favour, the next decision is whether to invest in a portable one or a permanently sited one. I argue for a permanent one on the grounds of expediency, efficiency and cost. Unless you take special care of them, after one or two uses, the movable metal ones with the bright paint, which look such a good buy in the store, can look like a rusty piece of scrap. The barbecue need not be too large or dominant. It need not be an eyesore. And, it can be easy to make.

SITING

Position it sensibly away from the doors of the house; there is no point in having all the smells of cooking wafting around inside. On the other hand, make it easy for access to the kitchen for fetching extra ingredients or making a dash for cover if unexpected rain suddenly arrives.

Smoke and heat may be a hazard – the smoke to you and neighbours; the heat especially to surrounding vegetation. Keep the construction away from plants or plants away from the barbecue.

DESIGNS

Space is needed to form the charcoal fire beneath a grill large enough to cook a generous amount of food in one go. It is useful to have a flat spot or table top next to the cooking area on which you can place tools and cooked food for dishing out onto plates. A more elaborate design might also incorporate a cupboard below the table to store cooking implements and charcoal. A hinged door will make it secure.

The basic permanent barbecue design below can be elaborated as seems sensible. The size can even be doubled, perhaps with two cooking places if you are a barbecue enthusiast with lots of friends to invite around. Depending on the site and the patio you may have the choice of adding a top over the barbecue to act as a cooker hood. This is normally a wooden frame fixed to the rear wall of the barbecue and hung with tiles like a roof.

BUILDING

■ Purchase or have made a barbecue set that consists of a grill, a firebed support and tools. The dimensions of these governs the brickwork. If bought ready made, the package may give construction details, probably close to the following.

■ Use old or new bricks that are proof against all weather.

■ Make the foundations some 10cm (4in) deep and a little wider to form a level concrete base.

■ Make the barbecue walls three sides of a square or rectangle. They can be a single brick thick, 10cm (4in), or double, approximately 22cm (9in) and the area will be about 3 bricks wide and 2 to 3 bricks deep.

■ After four or five courses, lay bricks projecting into the interior space by a couple of centimetres or so to support the fire cradle. Test the fit before cementing the bricks.

■ Lay a further two courses of brick before repeating the interior ledge, this time to support the grill.

■ Lay a further course before repeating the ledge again, this time to give the option of moving the grill higher.

WARNING

Barbecues can be dangerous. Read the following dos and don'ts

DON'T
■ *Do not allow any petrol, paraffin or other dangerous chemicals near the barbecue*
■ *Do not allow small children or pets near a working barbecue*

DO
■ *Always ensure the fire is fully out after use. Douse carefully with water*
■ *Wear sensible clothing near the barbecue – nothing loose that could catch fire*
■ *Store charcoal and other items where they will not be within reach of small children*
■ *Make sure the barbecue is safely sited away from the house and that there are no inflammable items nearby*
■ *Have a bucket of sand and another of water in a safe place close by*

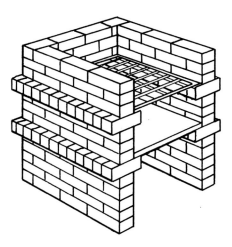

A course of bricks projecting into the interior space acts as a support for the fire cradle

■ Lay a final course to finish and neaten the appearance.

■ If you intend to install a roasting spit, design this final level to house the spit support.

An alternative design is to have bricks following around the front of the unit until the courses are high enough for the firebase. The resulting cavity is then filled in with rubble and grit or sand and a layer of firebricks laid to give a permanent base. It would be sensible to have just the slightest camber towards the front to shed rainwater.

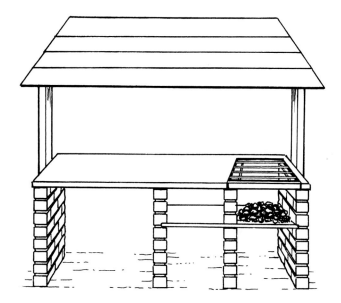

The support for the grill has now been added. At this stage you have the option of adding another ledge to give a higher grill position

ALTERNATIVE BARBECUE DESIGNS

Barbecues can be various shapes and sizes. The semi-circular one (left) makes an attractive feature and the square brick one (below) is temporary and can be dismantled after use

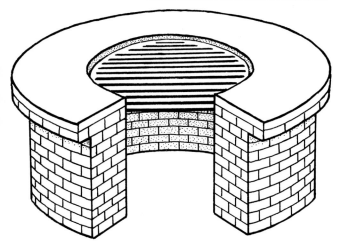

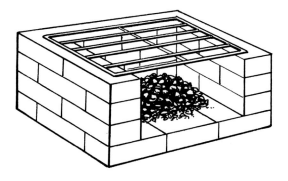

AUGUST

Late summer can be hot and dry and the patio becomes an oasis where a little shade from climbing plants is welcomed and the small pond with its sound of bubbling water gives some psychological sense of freshness and 'coolth'.

Wheel away the first large pots of lilies; their flowers are gone and, if allowed, they will be developing seed pods. Now the patio boasts the later-flowering kinds – those exotic Oriental hybrids with their intoxicating perfumes. Fresh greens of potted shrubs and plants, such as hostas and ferns, tucked into cooler shady spots, are there to be enjoyed and passion flowers excite wonder; in warm summers they provide a crop of interesting fruits as the blossoms fail.

In dry years, the grass will look parched and dry and the borders will benefit from early mulching with compost and shredded bark. Most of the herbaceous plants and shrubs will hold out well enough and careful watering and slow-release fertilizers ensure containers remain a picture. Water butts prove their worth – practical and ecologically sound! Gravelled areas close by the patio remain tidy and pleasing, with specimen plants well displayed. The gravel acts as a cool moisture-retaining mulch.

Before holidays begin, take time to plant some autumn-flowering crocuses and colchicums in beds by the patio or in containers. Some can go into rock beds where hardy Cyclamen hederifolium *will soon be sending up its first flowers, unchaperoned by leaves. Gardening is a matter of looking forward: the past is in the memory and on film, the present is fleeting, a springboard to future achievement.*

tasks
FOR THE
month

CHECKLIST

- Holiday precautions
- Buying bulbs
- Autumn-flowering bulbs
- Summer cuttings
- Growing agapanthus

HOLIDAY PRECAUTIONS

The main problem is likely to be keeping containers from getting dried out. Dropping large earthenware pots into plastic bags, with perhaps a small reservoir of water in the bottom, will help to reduce evaporation. If you have a system of automatic watering you can relax, but most of us must rely on friends to come in once or twice to give everything a thorough soaking. One real soaking is worth a dozen quick sprays with water, which will just dampen the plants on top of the soil. (Don't forget to bring back some duty-free as 'thank-yous'.)

Obviously you will need to soak all well before leaving home. And it is worth checking mulches on beds and topping them up if need be.

BUYING BULBS

The garden centres are already filling up with bulbs for the autumn bulb-buying festival. It is worth keeping an eye on them: some of the more unusual species are in short supply and stocks will quickly disappear. The sooner bulbs are planted – be it in containers or in beds – the better they will perform. Try to purchase the cleanest, largest bulbs without bruises or blemishes.

AUTUMN-FLOWERING BULBS

Top priority among the bulbs will be autumn-blooming crocuses and colchicums. They need planting fast. Sternbergias ought to be planted now, although they may not do all that much to start with. They are plants that like to get established and to be left alone until after several years they get overcrowded.

SUMMER CUTTINGS

It is surprising how expensive some bedding plants such as geraniums can be. It is well worth taking cuttings of these periodically and building up a small reserve ready for next year. The original plants may

LAYERING SHRUBS
Layering is the easiest way to propagate shrubs. Choose a long flexible stem near to the ground. Remove enough shoots to leave a bare section. Nick the bark on the lower side of this and treat with hormone rooting powder. Bury it in the soil, keeping it in place with a wire hoop. After 12 months cut through the connecting stem to separate the cutting from the parcel

get too large to handle by the end of the season.

If you have shrubs you want to propagate, the easiest, laziest way is layering. This is done by bending a branch down to the ground, scratching 5–7cm (2–3in) of the bark, treating this with hormone rooting powder, burying it in the soil and trapping it there with wire pegs or a brick. Leave it for twelve months before cutting through the stem between the parent and the new plant, then lift the rooted part and grow it on elsewhere. Alternatively,

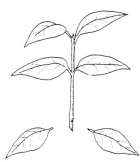

cuttings can be taken, either soft tissue ones or semi-ripe ones.

GROWING AGAPANTHUS

This traditional patio plant merits good treatment. Large pots of healthy green arching foliage topped by many tall stems of perhaps up to forty nodding trumpet flowers in shades of rich blue or white can be the focus of attention for several weeks in the high summer. Although the leaves and flowers give the impression that the plant may be bulbous, agapanthus in fact have thick perennial rootstocks which are usually hardy. Most of those for sale are Headbourne hybrids, often sold as unnamed seedlings but sometimes as named clones (see margin).

Tips for success

■ Grow in 20cm (8in) pots or larger, perhaps even half barrels: they make a mass of active roots.
■ The longer they can be left in

one pot the better as they do not relish root disturbance.
■ Give them soil with an open structure and plenty of humus.

■ Provide high potash feed once or twice a year — early spring, early summer.

■ Make sure they get all the sun available.

■ Ensure they get plenty of moisture while growing .

■ For complete safety from frost damage in winter, bury their crowns deeper under a thick mulch of shredded bark or similar material.

■ Split clumps every 2, 3, or 4 years.

AUTUMN-FLOWERING BULBS

bulb	flowers	height
Allium callimischon	white, spotted red	10cm (4in)
Amaryllis belladonna	pink	50cm (20in)
Colchicum autumnale 'Album'	white	15–20cm (6–8in)
Colchicum bivonae	pink-purple with darker speckling	10–15cm (4–6in)
Colchicum byzantinum	mauve	15–20cm (6–8in)
Colchicum speciosum	strong pink-purple	15–20cm (6–8in)
Colchicum speciosum 'Album'	outstanding white	15–20cm (6–8in)
Colchicum 'Lilac Wonder'	reliable, large, pink	15–20cm (6–8in)
Colchicum 'The Giant'	lilac-pink	15–20cm (6–8in)
Colchicum 'Waterlily'	pink-mauve, double-flowered curiousity	15–20cm (6–8in)
Crinum x *powellii*	pink	50–75cm (20–30in)
Crinum x *powellii* 'Albus'	white	50–75cm (20–30in)
Crocus banaticus	violet	2.5–8cm (1–3in)
Crocus kotschyanus	pinky mauve	8–10cm (3–4in)
Crocus nudiflorus	purple	2.5–8cm (1–3in)
Crocus pulchellus	lilac	2.5–8cm (1–3in)
Crocus speciosus	violet-blue, most reliable	4–8cm (1½–3in)
Crocus speciosus 'Albus'	good white	4–8cm (1½–3in)
Crocus speciosus 'Artabir'	pale blue inside, dark blue outside	4–8cm (1½–3in)
Crocus speciosus 'Oxonian'	deep violet	4–8cm (1½–3in)
Cyclamen cilicium	pink	10cm (4in)
Cyclamen cilicium album	white	10cm (4in)
Cyclamen hederifolium	pink	10cm (4in)
Cyclamen hederifolium album	white	10cm (4in)
Galanthus reginae-olgae	white	15cm (6in)
Leucojum autumnale	white	10cm (4in)
Nerine bowdenii	pink	45cm (18in)
Scilla autumnalis	lilac	8–10cm (3–4in)
Sternbergia lutea	yellow	3–15cm (1¼–6in)
Zephyranthes candida	white	15cm (6in)

AGAPANTHUS

All forms of agapanthus are attractive and worth considering for the patio garden. Narrow-leaved ones are hardy, broad-leaved ones are half-hardy.

A. **Headbourne Hybrids** – a series of strong-growing blues for a long season from midsummer **The following named hybrids are good selected forms:**
A. 'Alice Gloucester' – many crowded white flowers mid-into late summer, Ht. 50cm (20in) high heads
A. 'Ben Hope' – large umbels of dark blue flowers from late summer, Ht. 50cm (20in)
A. 'Dorothy Palmer' – free flowering, rich blue mid- to late summer, Ht. 1m (3ft)
A. 'Lilliput' – heads of small, dark blue bells in summer, Ht. 45cm (18in)
A. 'Loch Hope' – impressive large heads of deep blue flowers from late summer, Ht. 1–1.2m (3–4ft)

plants
OF THE
month

You'll have a riot of colour on the patio if you plant some of the bedding dahlias. They come in a combination of forms and colours: something to suit any colour scheme

BEDDING DAHLIA
(Dahlia 'Fabel'*)*

Dahlia 'Fabel' is a named clone, but you can raise all sorts of excellent dwarf bedding dahlias from seed and select the colours and forms that you like best, single flowers predominate among seedlings.

type	Tender, tuberous, herbaceous perennial
flowers	Double, vermilion-red, very prolific from early summer until the frosts
foliage	Fresh green, serrated margins, usually as three leaflets
height	35–80cm (15–32in)
spread	30–45cm (12–18in)
soil	Not fussy. In containers use a good compost with slow-release fertilizer or give a weekly dose of feed such as Phostrogen
site	Beds, borders or containers

care	Store tubers in cool frost-free conditions until planting, in well worked beds with extra humus, in mid-spring. Plant with 10cm (4in) of soil over tops. Take anti-slug precautions when sprouting
propagation	Divide tubers or take cuttings in late winter or early spring
relatives	*D.* 'Park Princess', with double, cactus-type, pink flowers, 70cm (28in); *D.* 'Border Princess', similar form, apricot-orange, 80cm (32in). *D.* 'Margaret Kleene' and sport *D.* 'Berliner Kleene', wide-petalled, rounded flowers in apricot-salmon and deep salmon-pink, sturdy 35cm (14in) high plants, very good in containers. *D.* Lilliput series, not much more than 30cm (12in) high, are single-flowered and crowded with bloom: 'Bambino', cream, 'Little John', gold, 'Red Riding Hood', scarlet, 'Maid Marion', pink, 'Tom Thumb', dark red, shading to a maroon-black centre

 ### SIBERIAN IRIS
(Iris sibirica)

This water-loving iris is a real trouble-free plant that looks deliciously cool in the sunny summer. It grows easily by or just in water, though it is also perfectly happy in a border away from water.

type	Clump-forming, herbaceous perennial

100

flowers   Vivid blue with some intricate darker and golden markings; several weeks in summer
foliage   Narrow, erect or slightly arching, fresh green, dies back in late autumn
height   60–90cm (24–36in)
spread   60–75cm (24–30in)
soil   Not fussy but enjoys moisture
site   Open spot in sun
care   Plant and leave
propagation   Easy from seed or division at the end of summer
relatives   Most named forms are rich blues, but there are others such as 'White Swirl', 'Sparkling Rose', mauve-pink, 'Butter and Sugar', creamy yellow, and 'Silver edge', violet-edged white

SMALL WATER LILY

(Nymphaea pygmaea alba)

Water is always magic, but with the water lilies opening the enchantment increases. This one is among the smallest and can be grown in very small pools or even in tubs.

type   Perennial water plant
flowers   White, 3.5cm (1¹/₂in) across, with bright green sepals
foliage   Floating, small, round pads
spread   50cm (20in)
site   Any water up to 30cm (12in) deep
care   Plant in wire- or plastic-mesh baskets with rich heavy soil topped with gravel
propagation   Divide roots at end of winter
relatives   Most water lilies are larger but there are some small ones such as the yellow-flowered *N. pygmaea* 'Helvola'

LATE DUTCH HONEYSUCKLE

(Lonicera periclymenum 'Serotina'*)*

This is a very free-flowering, fragrant version of the native woodbine, with darker, later flowers.

type   Deciduous, woody, twining climber
flowers   Long tubed, deep wine-coloured and buff-gold, pink inside; mid- to late summer
foliage   Oval, mid-green, grey-green below
height   8m (24ft)
site   Sun or shade. Up trees, trellis, walls or pergolas
soil   Any fertile, well-drained soil
care   Carefree. Prune away awkward stems, dead wood and to keep within your chosen limits
propagation   Easily rooted from layered branches
relatives   *L. periclymenum* 'Graham Thomas', white summer blossom soon maturing to rich buff-yellow

NON-CLIMBING HONEYSUCKLES
Shrubby, non-climbing honeysuckles are also available. They include L. × purpusii 'Winter Beauty', which has very sweetly-scented white flowers in winter and early spring, and L. nitida, which does not flower but has tiny evergreen leaves and is excellent for hedging

practical project

INCLUDING WATER FEATURES

FOLIAGE PLANTS FOR WATER MARGINS

Arum lily (*Zantedeschia aethiopica*)
Broad buckler fern (*Dryopteris dilitata*)
Giant lily (*Cardiocrinum giganteum*)
Gunnera manicata, has huge leaves so use only where there is plenty of space
G. scabra, much smaller and more spreading
Hostas, all kinds
Ligularias, in variety
Peltiphyllum peltatum
Rheum palmatum
Rogersia, various
Royal fern (*Osmunda regalis*)
Skunk cabbage (*Lysichiton americanus*)

Almost every garden design is enhanced by water. Certainly on or near the patio it makes big magic, without necessarily involving huge engineering feats.

DESIGN CONSIDERATIONS

Site
Where possible, it is best to site the water feature quite close to the patio, where it can be seen and heard, especially if the water is moving. With timber patios, the decking can be made to overlap the edge of a pool of water for an at sea, maritime effect.

It is unusual to site large pools close to the house but it can been done very successfully, almost like a moat . However, it is very enjoyable to look over a stretch of lawn towards a sheet of water with attendant vegetation. And, the further from the house, the less formal the water need be, perhaps being a real wildlife habitat.

Shape
Even close to the house, a pool can be informal in outline although squared-off patios tend to demand formally shaped and constructed pools. Oblong, rather than square, seems happier, but a circular one could be equally effective.

Depth
Water plants require differing depths of water. Marginal plants will grow in wet soil at the edge of pools; some will not object to having water over their bases, others thrive in depths of up to 20cm (8in) of water but some popular water lilies really need 45cm (18in) depth. *(Continued on page 104.)*

practical project

INCLUDING WATER FEATURES (continued)

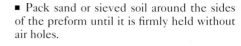

MARGINAL PLANTS PRIMARILY FOR FLOWERS

Astilbes, various, white, pink, red plumes
Globe flower *(Trollius europaeus)*, lemon-yellow
Himalayan cowslip *(Primula florindae)*, pale yellow
***Iris ensata* (syn. *I. kaempferi*),** various, white, blue, violet, purple, mauve, pink and bicolours
I. laevigata, deep blue and purple
I. pseudacorus, golden
Marsh marigold *(Caltha palustris)*, golden
Marsh marigold, double (*Caltha palustris* 'Plena'), rich yellow
Monkey musk *(Mimulus guttatus)*, various, yellow, orange, red, often spotted
Primula, all candelabra types
Primula japonica, various colours
P. pulverulenta, many wine colours
Purple loosestrife *(Lythrum salicaria)*, wine-red

SMALL POOLS

Space may be limited, but even a small pool has a beneficial effect out of all proportion to its size. The easiest to install is one lined by a preformed mould. Try not to have less than two square metres (yards) of surface water. Maintaining a pool in good health is difficult if it is very tiny; the temperature of the water and its chemical content can vary dramatically in short periods of time. This causes difficulties for animals and plants and may stimulate the formation of algae, blanket weed and other undesirables.

Procedure

■ Excavate a hole larger than the preform and fit it in position so that the top reaches just under the surrounding ground level.

■ Check that the bottom is level, adjusting the hole until the preform is sitting evenly on the base.

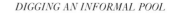

■ Pack sand or sieved soil around the sides of the preform until it is firmly held without air holes.

■ Fill with water.

■ Cover the top of the preform overlaps with turf, rocks, stones or gravel.

■ Introduce plants to the deeper centre and to the shelved sides.

FOUNTAINS AND GUSHES

Keep things simple. A single jet that breaks evenly is much more pleasing than a multi-faceted series of jets at varying angles. Depending on your scheme, you may choose from a traditional vertical fountain jet or a more modern angled one, which will allow the light to catch the water. A series of boulders and stones beneath for the water to fall on is effective. Wall-mounted features can be

DIGGING AN INFORMAL POOL

Use a garden hose to mark out the pond site. If you are not using a preform cut ledges during excavation to position plants on later

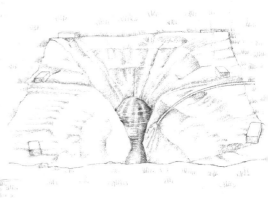

As the pond fills the lining will stretch into place (above).

Trim off any excess liner and disguise the edges with gravel or rocks and plants

made to issue a jet of varying strengths.

There is no need for a fountain to enjoy the sound of water running. Water can be piped to a series of boulders and stones, to gush forth and then be collected below and sent around the circuit again.

All moving water can be governed by an electric pump with a switch in the house.

MAINTENANCE

■ Electrical parts should be installed to require minimum maintenance but must be checked regularly to forestall accidents.

■ Pools will need clearing of dead leaves and detritus before the winter.

PLANTS FOR WATER UP TO 20CM (8IN) DEEP
Golden club *(Orontium aquaticum)*, yellow
Lysichiton americanus, golden spathes
L. camtschatcensis, white spathes
Pickerel *(Pontaderia cordata)*, purple-blue flowers, arrowhead leaves
Water fringe *(Nymphoides peltata)*, golden flowers, round leaves

OXYGENATING PLANTS
Canadian pondweed *(Elodea canadensis)*
Lagarosiphon major, one of the best
Milfoil, spiked *(Myriophyllum spicatum)*
Milfoil, whorled *(M. verticillatum)*
Water crowfoot *(Ranunculus acquatilis)*
Water violet *(Hottonia palustris)*

WATER LILIES
Nymphaea alba, white, depth to 90cm (36in)
***N.* 'Escarboucle'**, outstanding red, depth to 45cm (18in)
***N.* × *marliacea* 'Chromatella'**, yellow, depth to 90cm (36in)
N. odorata, white, depth 15–30cm (6–12in)
N. pygmaea alba, white, depth 15–30cm (6–12in)
***N.* 'Sunrise'**, golden, depth over 90cm (36in)

INFORMAL POOL

SEPTEMBER

As high summer moves towards the autumn, the leaves of some trees begin to colour up, though it is next month that the full scale performance is given, followed by leaf fall. In the garden, there is a swing of emphasis towards the flowers of autumn: Michaelmas daisies, chrysanthemums and dahlias; but summer is not done yet. There are days, perhaps weeks, when the weather may be as pleasant and bright as any that high summer provided, and relaxing on the patio can be as pleasing as ever.

The fragrance of barbecues is still wafting through the land and there is still time to make good use of equipment and the patio before the cooler weather arrives. Plan a party for the weekend and hope the weather smiles.

Plenty of colour is still supplied by containers and annuals, although some have passed their best: the lobelia has faded away, but begonias, pelargoniums, busy lizzies and petunias are surprisingly good. It proves worth doing a thorough job deadheading (or bribing the children to do it) earlier on. As it is time to plan for winter and spring displays, with bulbs, winter pansies, heathers and ivies, it is prudent to clear some of the more weary summer containers and replant them with fresh specimens.

The rock bed beside the patio is becoming interesting again, with the wonderful hardy cyclamen blooming prolifically and an overnight appearance of leafless crocus flowers. Against the house walls, clumps of Nerine bowdenii and perhaps the even more flamboyant Amaryllis belladonna provide an eye-catching touch of freshness and theatrical magic. Higher on the walls and along the patio there may be roses still blooming, but now is the time to eye the ripening bunches of grapes and wonder about treading them in the bath!

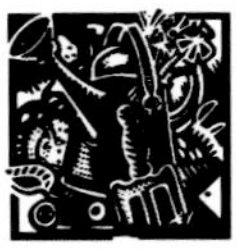

tasks FOR THE *month*

BULBS FOR POTS AND OTHER CONTAINERS

Crocus, large-flowered
Hyacinths: protect from frost
***Iris reticulata* group**
***I.* danfordiae,** yellow 10cm (4in)
***I.* 'George',** purple 15cm (6in)
***I.* 'Joyce',** blue 15cm (6in)
***I.* 'Harmony',** blue 15cm (6in)
Muscari azureum, sky blue 8cm (3in)
***M. azureum* 'Album',** white 8cm (3in)
***M. botryoides* 'Album',** white 15cm (6in)
***Narcissus* 'February Gold',** yellow 20–30cm (8–12in)
***N.* 'Jenny',** white and cream 20–30cm (8–12in)
***N.* 'Jumblie',** yellow 15–20cm (6–8in)
***N.* 'Tête à Tête',** yellow 15–20cm (6–8in)
Snowdrops *(Galanthus)*
Tulips, *kaufmanniana* hybrids
***T.* 'Electra',** double, early, red 25cm (10in)
***T. greigii* hybrids**
***T.* 'Mr Van der Hoef',** yellow 25cm (10in)
***T.* 'Peach Blossom',** rich pink 25cm (10in)

CHECKLIST

- Planting bulbs
- Saving half-hardy plants
- Harvesting seed
- Trimming hedges

PLANTING BULBS

This is one of the busiest seasons for bulb planting. If you are aiming for a super-spring, it is a good idea to concentrate on early flowers. Having already dealt with autumn-blooming bulbs last month (see p98), now is also the time to think of winter. (See list in the margin.)

In beds, dig over soil, add a sprinkle of general fertilizer and then plant your bulbs in bold groups. Avoid straight lines of bulbs, they look artificial and, as sure as bulbs are bulbs, one in the middle of the row will fail or get broken to ruin the effect.

Planting depths are below: try not to skimp on these.

Bulbs in pots and containers

It is not too early to plant up pots and containers for spring. Once planted, some pots can be left outside – sunk in a plunge bed if severe winter weather threatens – others can be kept cool for eight weeks and then be brought in to a touch of warmth, for example, in a greenhouse with the heating only coming on when the temperature falls to near frost. With only this slight warmth, these bulbs will bloom a month earlier than those outside.

Use varieties of daffodils and tulips with sturdy stems and resilient flowers that can be expected to make a real impact (see margin for suggestions).

Doubling up

A double layer of bulbs will help produce a substantial crowded display. Follow this procedure:

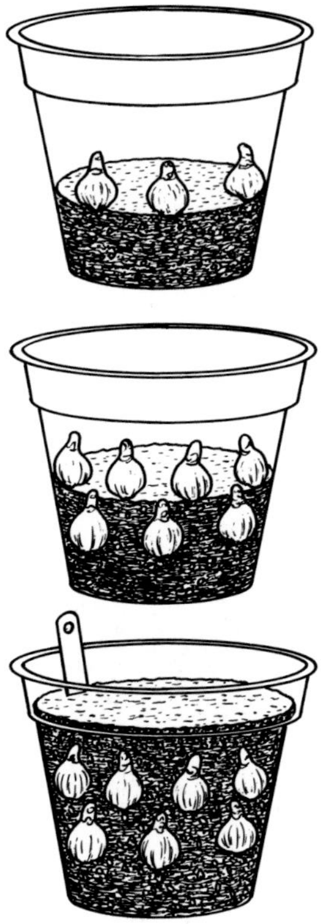

BULB PLANTING DEPTHS

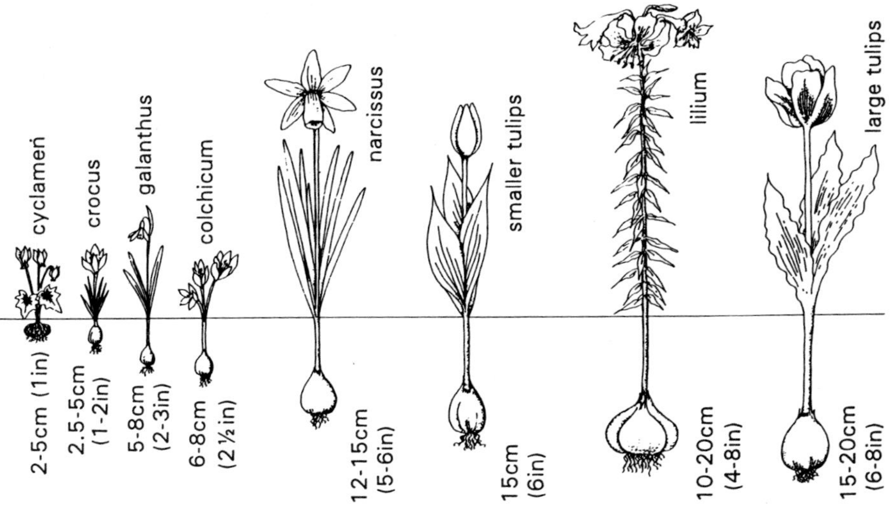
cyclamen
2-5cm (1in)
crocus
2.5-5cm (1-2in)
galanthus
5-8cm (2-3in)
colchicum
6-8cm (2½in)
narcissus
12-15cm (5-6in)
smaller tulips
15cm (6in)
lilium
10-20cm (4-8in)
large tulips
15-20cm (6-8in)

After flowering, the bulbs can be planted out in the garden to gather strength and provide colour in future years. It is unwise to try the same bulbs in containers for a second year.

SAVING HALF-HARDY PLANTS

Frosts are going to come — next month probably. Take geranium cuttings now and think of other plants as well, especially the osteospermums and argyranthemums, such as *A.* 'Jamaica Primrose', if you did not take cuttings of their non-flowering shoots last month.

Follow this procedure:

■ Choose healthy shoots

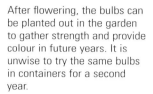

■ Using a sharp implement, cut off lower leaves

■ Trim cutting base cleanly at a leaf node

■ Dust the base with hormone rooting powder and insert in pot of equal mix of peat and grit or perlite

■ Keep just moist and cover with polythene, not touching the cuttings

HARVESTING SEED

Seed is not very cheap and many gardeners prefer to save their own. This works well with some plants, but it is useless with F1 hybrids, which will not come 'true'. Some simple annuals, such as love-in-the-mist (*Nigella*) will make too good a job of seeding themselves. Armies of such seedlings need to be hoed down leaving just the odd few.

Collect ripe seeds just before the plant sheds them, or tie a paper bag over the seedheads *in situ*. In a dry place, shake out seed onto a sheet of clean paper to separate off the chaff and then store them in a dry envelope with the plant name clearly printed. Keep seed cool and dry until sowing. (See margin for suggestions.)

TRIMMING HEDGES

With a powered trimmer, cutting the hedge is simple, and the more often it is undertaken, the neater and denser the hedge becomes. As hedges close to the patio are likely to be miniature ones — box, *Lonicera nitida*, berberis or heathers — it is best to aim at an even cover of foliage from top to earth level. Sloping the sides somewhat inwards towards the top helps to achieve this. It is usual for box to have a square top but lonicera can be brought to a very narrow, almost pointed, top.

Hedges of dwarf lavender need to be kept under review, they may not be dealt with so drastically with hedge-trimmers, but any legginess needs to be avoided so fairly frequent snipping with secateurs or shears is sensible. Do the last trim as the flowers begin to look untidy (see list of suggested plants in margin).

BULBS FOR PLANTING OUTSIDE:

Crocuses
Crown imperials (*Fritillaria imperialis*)
Daffodils, all types
Iris, Dutch hybrids
Iris, English hybrids
Iris, dwarf reticulata types
Lilies, all types
Snake's head fritillaries (*Fritillaria meleagris*)
Snowdrops
Tulips, all types

SEED SAVING
Save all sorts of seeds to sow now or later. Avoid F1 hybrids as they will not come 'true'.

Calendula
Iris, various
Lilies, various
Poppy (*Papaver*)
Primula various
Love-in-the-mist (*Nigella*)

HEDGING PLANTS FOR AROUND PATIO
Berberis thunbergii 'Atropurpurea Nana' – and other dwarf forms
Buxus sempervirens 'Suffructicosa'
Erica carnea – for a low edging hedge
E. erigena
Euonymus fortunei vars.
E. japonicus vars.
Lavandula angustifolia 'Hidcote'
Lonicera nitida
L. n. 'Baggesen's Gold'

DIVISION OF PLANTS
Herbaceous plants can be divided this month or next

plants
OF THE
month

KOREAN CHRYSANTHEMUM
(*Chrysanthemum koreanum* 'Fanfare' (F1 hybrids)

Korean chrysanthemums are hardy except in really extraordinarily severe winters. Like the older varieties, they have a very free-flowering habit, but produce double flowers. Seed is usually sold as mixed colours but in subsequent years you can take cuttings of those that produce favourite colours.

type	Half-hardy herbaceous perennial
flowers	Double pompoms, 8cm (3in) across, in mixed colours and large numbers from late summer until frosts. Blooms earlier in cool summers
foliage	Small, typical chrysanthemum leaves
height	75cm (30in)
spread	45–60cm (18–24in)
site	Beds or large containers
soil	Fertile soil with plenty of humus and fertilizer
care	Sow seed at the end of winter, prick out, plant out after the danger of frost is past. Alternatively, overwinter plants or take early cuttings and plant out in late spring. In mild areas, plants may be left out over winter

propagation	Divide and replant in spring
relatives	*C. indicum* 'Charm' (early mixed) is a range of very floriferous 'cushion' chrysanthemums, 30–50cm (12–20in) high. The 5cm (2in) flowers, in a wide range of shades, smother the foliage from late summer until really hard frosts, making mounds of colour

GOLDEN GRASS
(*Hakonechloa macra* 'Aureola')

This is one of the best of the newly popular grasses. It is not a rampant grower but it looks good as a small plant and once it has formed a thick mat of roots, it produces an explosion of foliage. It is ideal for growing in a container, where it will make a focal point of cascading yellow in the growing months before turning to rusty-bronzes in the autumn.

type	Hardy perennial variegated grass, with compact rhizomes
flowers	Chestnut-coloured flower spikes may or may not appear in early autumn and can then persist through winter
foliage	Narrow, arching, yellow, with thin green stripes. Old age and winter turns leaves to rusty brown. New growth starts in early spring
height	25–40cm (10–16in)
spread	30–50cm (12–20in)
site	Beds, borders, or makes a splendid container plant Prefers an open site but can be grown in shade
soil	Best in light sandy soil that is not allowed to dry out
care	Plant in early spring. A fairly substantial plant is needed for a container as it grows slowly, but it can be grown on in containers for as long as necessary
propagation	Split larger clumps in spring

NERINE
(*Nerine bowdenii*)

Nerine bowdenii is the only reliably hardy species of this South African genus, but of its hardiness you need have no qualms at all. For the first year or so, the newly planted bulbs may look a little thin, with only one or two flower stems, but then it gets going and is prolific; it will be marvellous for the next decade or two or three . . .

type	Hardy bulb

flowers Umbels of 6–12 flowers, each with six petals, wavy margined at tips, in a trumpet that becomes very wide. Brilliant rich pink

foliage Narrow, strap-shaped, polished; usually disappear some weeks before the flower stems appear

height 40–60cm (16–24in)

site Best in a warm sunny spot, often planted near a sheltered wall. Can also be be grown as a long-term tenant of an earthenware pot

soil Open-textured, well-drained. In pots, use a sandy mix

care Plant these long bulbs with their necks level with, or only very lightly covered by, soil. Try to leave undisturbed until clumps become very overcrowded

propagation Bulbs increase in number quickly. After three or four years clumps can be lifted in the summer, bulbs separated and replanted immediately

relatives *N. bowdenii* 'Pink Triumph' makes a robust plant with well-coloured, good-sized flowers

MICHAELMAS DAISY
(*Aster amellus* 'Violet Queen')

Like all *A. amellus* cultivars, 'Violet Queen' is immune to the mildew that often spoils other autumn-flowering asters. This is one of the better cultivars making a tidy plant, and having richly coloured flowers. You could try saving seed and raising some new individuals with slightly different flowers, something I have done very successfully. Sow seed in late autumn or spring.

type Hardy herbaceous perennial

flowers Sprays of many, open daisy flowers of dark violet purple in early autumn; last for several weeks. Yellow-stamened centres add considerably to the effect

foliage Very dark green, oval

height 25–45cm (10–18in)

spread 25–45cm (10–18in)

site Best in a sunny, well-drained spot

soil Fertile soil that does not dry out

care Easy

propagation Split plants or take cuttings in spring. Do not try this in autumn, you could lose your plants

relatives *A. amellus* 'King George' is similar, perhaps a shade taller. *A. amellus* 'Sonia' is pink-flowered

RED HOT POKER
(*Kniphofia* 'Little Maid')

A red hot poker that is neither red nor hot, most kniphofias and is ideal for growing near the patio, with its slender, not over-dominant foliage and long succession of flower spikes. Try positioning some of its rather larger relatives a little further away as they, too, are durable in bloom: the largest will show up from a distance of a hundred yards.

type Hardy herbaceous perennial

flowers Slender stems with long heads of outward-pointing creamy yellow flowers that then tend to droop and bleach to pale cream

foliage Typical *Kniphofia* foliage is grass-like: miniaturized and narrow

height 40–60cm (16–24in)

spread 50–60cm (20–24in)

site Sun or semi-shade, towards the front of a bed or border

soil Fertile, with plenty of humus

care Easy plant best left undisturbed for two or three seasons before being propagated in early spring. In bleak areas can be given winter protection by mulching with shredded bark or compost

propagation Best early spring but early flowering kinds may be split in late summer. Old plants can be made into several parts by using two forks driven into the clump back to back and riven apart. Make sure that plants do not dry out

relatives Most kniphofias make much larger, taller plants. *K.* 'Percy's Pride', one such, is upright with large lime-yellow flowerheads, 1m (3ft) high, and healthy, narrow foliage

practical project

MAKING USEFUL GARDEN FEATURES

MAKING A BIRD TABLE OR BIRD BATH

Different types of birds tend to feed and bathe at different heights and situations. The true ground feeders are difficult to persuade to use tables or baths more than a very few inches above the ground. So to satisfy all tastes you need at least two stations; three or four would be better. This will allow for some being on or near the ground and others about 75cm (30in) high. Simple structures will serve: the birds are more interested in the food and their safety than aesthetic considerations, and to our eyes a simple artifact can look better than an elaborate construction.

Make a very simple bird table of paving stones arranged as shown with the base and the table top joined by a field drain pipe or two, filled with concrete with some crushed chicken wire for reinforcement and making sure that the top and base are securely attached.

A round table top is easily made by using a dustbin lid, or similar, as a mould for the concrete mix. Construct a bird bath the same way but remember to make a depression. This can be set into the concrete using the bottom of a round plastic container.

MAKING A BIRD TABLE

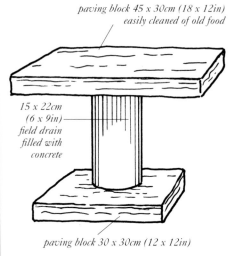

paving block 45 x 30cm (18 x 12in) easily cleaned of old food

15 x 22cm (6 x 9in) field drain filled with concrete

paving block 30 x 30cm (12 x 12in)

MAKING A BIRD BATH

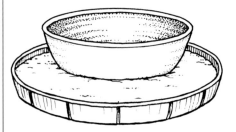

A dustbin lid is used as a mould for the bird bath. It is filled with concrete and a plastic bowl pushed into the centre to make a depression to hold the water

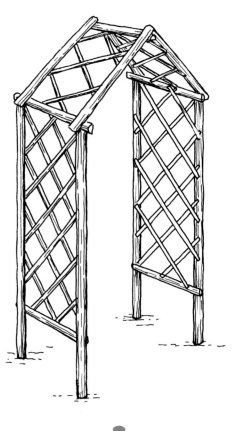

MAKING A RUSTIC ARCH

You can buy rustic poles from most wood yards. Some will strip off the bark and run a saw down two sides to give you straight surfaces to work with. Wood yards also supply poles that have been split down the centre to have a cross section as a half sphere – useful for the decorative interior supports. The idea is to make the arch in four parts, two sides and two sloping tops, and then join all pieces together at the site. The dimensions given allow for the inserting of 30cm (12in) of the uprights into the ground – probably best into metal housings or secured by concrete.

First make the two sides using the full-sized poles with one straightened edge facing inwards. Add the decorative criss-cross pattern using the split pole wood, with the flat surfaces facing inwards. Remember to allow an overlap for the two roofing parts and arrange for their joining surfaces to be at an appropriate angle, the interior angle span being something in the region of 135°. Large nails are going to do the main joining work so drill pilot holes in appropriate places.

MAKING A SMALL ROCK GARDEN

A well made rock garden using decent sized rocks, properly laid, can make a very pleasing feature close to the patio and is easily planted so that it is interesting at all times.

■ Outline area, perhaps an oval shape, and remove turf or a few centimetres of topsoil.

■ Dig or rotovate area and work in grit/hardcore to improve drainage. Lay drainage pipes to a lower area if poorly drained.

■ Rake over area to produce some light contouring. If only a few square metres are being used, arrange one high point, but if you are being more generous with space have a secondary highish spot with an intervening valley. Certainly arrange a low area where plants wanting a little more moisture and possibly shade can be accommodated.

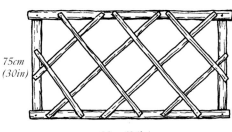

ROOF

75cm
(30in)

90cm (36in)

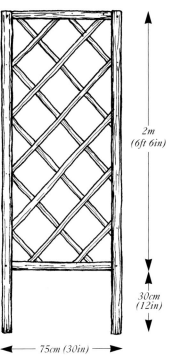

SIDE

2m
(6ft 6in)

30cm
(12in)

75cm (30in)

■ Use a limited number of large rocks rather than a welter of small ones. By abutting two middle-sized rocks, an impression of considerable size may be gained.

■ Arrange rocks so that they look as near as possible to a natural outcrop piercing the surface. Have strata lines running parallel.

■ Place rocks securely and infill with a gritty mix of soil between: 2 parts healthy loam to 1 part of humus and 1 part of grit is a basic mix that suits most rock garden plants.

■ Plant up with mix of dwarf conifers, creeping plants like thymes, clump-forming ones such as primulas and dwarf dianthus, foliage kinds such as sempervivums and small spring and autumn bulbs.

■ Tidy surface by spreading a layer of washed gravel or rock chippings.

Profile of contouring in the rock garden, showing a high spot and a shallow valley

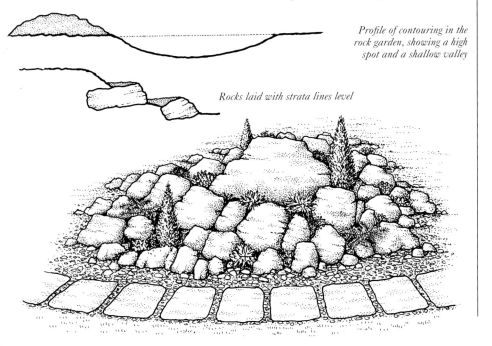

Rocks laid with strata lines level

OCTOBER

This is a sweet-sour time. There are magic days, starting with autumn mists and soon becoming golden with warm sunshine lighting up a landscape full of autumn colour. There are other dull, wet days when we have to accept that summer is over and winter is approaching. Maximize the positive features of autumn. The Michaelmas daisies come to a glorious climax, both the Aster novi-belgii *kinds, that repay all the time spent spraying against mildew, and the more amenable, mildew-resistant forms of A.* amellus, *as well as the almost ridiculously floriferous, small-flowered A.* ericoides *and A.* cordifolius, *with their crowded galaxies of twinkling stars. Planted so that they can be admired from the patio, they form one of the themes of autumn. Leaf colour is another. On the walls, Virginia creepers turn fantastic shades before frosts help them come tumbling down. Rakes and brushes busy themselves collecting the pools of fallen leaves to convert into compost: I have one of the very useful vacuum machines for collecting loose leaves and regard it as one of my better investments – there are plenty of other tools hanging in the shed that soon outlived first enthusiasm. Thus thoughts turn to clearing out the shed before winter and making room for garden furniture that needs to be stored away.*

*Keats said his bit about mists and autumn fruitfulness (*To Autumn*): the mists have come; the fruit is also here. Berries crowd the stems of pyracanthas and crab apples have been decorative for weeks. Cotoneasters are well-berried and will still be so for months to come if the birds do not attack them: perhaps there are fewer berry-eating birds or the milder winters provide alternative foods. Hopefully hollies will produce for Christmas. They have plenty of coloured berries already but while other berries may linger, the birds seem to take holly berries the day before they are due to be cut for decoration. Can it be thought transference?*

tasks

FOR THE

month

**HERBACEOUS PLANTS
FOR DIVIDING NOW**

Achilleas, all forms, at
beginning of the month or
spring
Aster novi-belgii, all forms tall
and dwarf. Note: ***Aster amellus***
forms should be left until
spring
Campanulas, strong forms in
autumn, others in spring
Deadnettle *(Lamium)*
Doronicum 'Spring Beauty' and
others
Geraniums, strong forms now,
others in spring
***Helenium* 'Moerheim Beauty'** and
others
Inula hookeri and others
Peonies
Polygonums
Ranunculus, strong forms
Solidago virgaurea var. *minuta*
***S.* 'Goldenmosa'**
***S.* 'Laurin'**

**Most other herbaceous plants that
can be divided are best dealt with
in spring**

CHECKLIST

- ☐ Divide plants
- ☐ Winter and Spring containers
- ☐ Checking wall plant supports
- ☐ Tending ivies
- ☐ Tidying rock gardens and raised beds
- ☐ Making leafmould

WINTER AND SPRING CONTAINERS

Some containers may already
be bursting with bulbs planted
last month. There is still time
for others to make growth, but
winter effects need
considering too. Some of the
spring-flowering bulb-filled
ones can look very empty now
and would be a lot better
supplemented with a few
trailing ivies. These are cheap
and effective, especially the
golden- and silver-variegated
forms. Or you can try crowding
a few pots or hanging baskets
with winter-flowering pansies;
either mix colours or plant
individual containers with
single colours – almost
always more effective.

Another ploy is to plant up a
container with winter-flowering
heathers – using good-sized
specimens – which can then be
planted out into the garden
when winter is over.

DIVIDE PLANTS

As you are tidying up beds
and borders around the patio
you may come across clumps
of plants that have become
overlarge or need
rejuvenating. These can be
divided to create extra stock
for replanting, putting in other
parts of the garden or even
giving away.

How its done

- ■ Cut away top growth.

- ■ Dig up and lift clump.

- ■ Remove it on to sacking or
a plastic sheet (1).

- ■ Make the first division by
inserting two forks back to
back and forcing them apart.
Repeat until you have as many
reasonable sized plants as you
need (2).

- ■ Using only the outer, more

lively, pieces replant firmly in
redug soil (3 and 4).

■ Discard any surplus — and
do not forget to return the
extra fork you borrowed from
your neighbour!

CHECKING WALL PLANT SUPPORTS

Choose a fine day to get
prepared for winter winds by
checking all the supports used
for plants, especially those on
the walls. Where trelliswork
is fixed to walls by screws
into rawlplugs, make sure
that the plugs have not
worked loose — a possibility if
the mortar is not all that
strong. Examine the ties and
stakes around shrubs and
trees still needing support to
ensure trunk or branches are
not getting chafed against
posts.
　　If you have not already
fixed trellis or wires to the
wall for plant supports
consider doing it now while
climbing plants are dormant.
A permanent system of
support is much more
satisfactory than hammering
individual nails into the wall
and tying growth in; it also
does less damage to the wall
(see also p140).

TENDING IVIES

Ivies, especially brightly
coloured ones, can be very
good value through the
winter. Make the most of
them by removing any dead
leaves and cutting away loose
twigs.

TIDYING ROCK GARDENS AND RAISED BEDS

Through the autumn leaves
will be falling everywhere.
They are easily worked into a
border, but can be a threat in
a rock garden where they may
cover plants and start rotting
problems. In these areas,

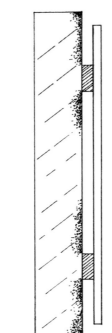

TWO IDEAS FOR PLANT SUPPORTS FOR WALLS

*Left: Attach wooden trellis
to wall-mounted wooden
blocks so that it can be
unscrewed and laid down
for maintenance or exten-
sive pruning*

*Right: Using 'vine eyes'
(metal screws with holes in
flattened tops) stretch wires
horizontally. Tension can
be increased using tension
screws. Climbing growth is
tucked in behind the wires
or attached to them*

remove fallen leaves as soon
as possible and topdress beds
with gravel, compost or
shredded bark to make them
tidy for the winter.

MAKING LEAFMOULD

One of the most plant-friendly
of humus forms and caviare to
woodland plants, you can
never have too much
leafmould. It can be
incorporated into potting and
other soil and can also be
used as a mulch. All leaves
are good, but oak and beech
are exceptional. It is often
best to mix all types together.

■ Collect fallen leaves. If
possible put dry material
through a shredder; it will rot
down much quicker.

■ While you are at it get out
the extension ladder and
remove leaves from the
guttering. Make sure the ladder
is secure, preferably with a
reliable partner footing it.

Leaves on the lawn can be
shredded into bits with a
rotary grass cutter.

■ Pile collected leaves in a
corner, contained by oak
palings or chicken wire.

■ Turn after six months.

■ Usable in 12–15 months.

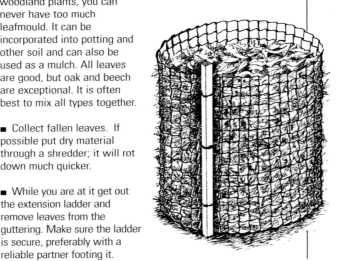

plants
OF THE
month

▼ **DWARF BAMBOO**

(Sasaella ramosa, syn. *Arundinaria vagans)*

This is an easy bamboo – too easy if you do not keep an eye on it, as it can be somewhat invasive. However, it adds a touch of atmosphere to the patio and it can be grown safely in a container.

type	Evergreen bamboo
flowers	Not to be expected
foliage	Tough, dark shining green, narrow, slightly less than horizontally held from slender, erect stems
height	45–90cm (18–36in)
spread	90cm (36in) but several times this after several years if not checked
soil	Not fussy
site	Container or a bed where its propensity to invade neighbouring territory can be held in check
care	Keep out of severe winds that could batter foliage
propagation	Increase by division in spring
relatives	Other bamboos are usually much larger: graceful *Phyllostachys nigra* has bending canes that become black by the third year and dainty foliage in masses; but stems can reach well over 6m (20ft). *Arundinaria viridistriata* has golden and green variegated foliage, 75–90cm (30–36in)

▲ **VIRGINIA CREEPER**

(Parthenocissus henryana)

Excellent on a shaded wall or growing through a deciduous tree, such as an apple or a pear, this is one of the most attractive of foliage climbers. On a wall it benefits from the help of trellis or wires. It is at its best from spring till the autumn when the foliage takes on a thousand brilliant fiery shades.

type	Deciduous climber with tendrils
flowers/fruit	Insignificant itsy-bitsy yellowish clusters, followed by miniature black grapes attractive to birds
foliage	Divided into three or five serrated leaflets to 15cm (6in) long. Polished green with a bronzy cast and with paler pinkish veining; very colourful in autumn

height	Almost any height with support, say 10m (30ft) or more
soil	Not fussy
site	Most effective grown through a deciduous tree or on a wall
care	Easy. A new young plant gets away quicker if tied into support as the new shoots grow
propagation	Can be propagated by cuttings or layers
relatives	*P. quinquefolia*, the true Virginia creeper, has five leaflets of less polished green and wonderful autumn colours. It is capable of climbing 20m (60ft)

COLCHICUM

(Colchicum 'Lilac Wonder'*)*

Provided this is planted where its large spring leaves will not annoy, this is a real first-rate garden plant looking very fresh and unusual in the autumn.

type	Corm
flowers	Very clean shaped, rich lilac-pink, long globes; mid-autumn
foliage	Large, rounded leaves, almost like dark green hostas appear in spring and die down before summer
height	15–20cm (6–8in) in bloom, 20–30cm (8–12in) in leaf
site	Sunny, open site best, but remember the large leaves which may look better between shrubs
soil	Open-structured with humus
care	Plant newly purchased corms in late summer. Cover corms with 7–8cm (3in) of soil
propagation	Lift when crowded – every other year to get maximum increase – in late spring. Divide and replant immediately in freshly worked soil
relatives	All single ones are to be preferred above *C.* 'Waterlily', an ugly double. *C.* 'The Giant' is very large with rich mauve-pink flowers fading to white centres. *C. speciosum* 'Album' is a magnificent form

DWARF CONIFER

(Thuja occidentalis 'Rheingold'*)*

This cone-shaped conifer is pleasing as a small specimen as well as a mature one and is furnished to the ground with rather loosely displayed stems of golden yellow and light green foliage, becoming bronzed in winter. It is slow-growing but can eventually reach perhaps 4m (12ft) high so plant small specimens where this size will be appropriate, unless you are willing to jettison the plant when it outgrows its site.

type	Evergreen, slow-growing conifer
flowers	None
foliage	Fresh golden yellow and light green, bronzed in winter
height	Takes 15–20 years to reach 2–4m (10–12ft)
spread	Almost as broad as it is high
soil	Not fussy
site	Bed, border, rock bed or container
care	Plant to take account of its eventual height and spread. Keep neighbouring plants at a distance so that its shape is kept well displayed
propagation	Summer cuttings from low on the bush. They can take some months to root
relatives	*T. orientalis* 'Aurea Nana', 60cm (2ft) high and wide, has very neat tightly packed vertical fans of golden-flushed green foliage, becoming bronzed in winter

AUTUMN CROCUS

(Crocus speciosus)

There are a number of autumn-flowering crocuses; this species is the most vigorous, free flowering and showy. A patch can make one of the best pictures of the autumn.

type	Corm
flowers	Fat, long globes of pale violet-blue with fragmented orange stigmata; early autumn
foliage	Narrow, grassy leaves with a central white stripe appear well after flowers, in winter or early spring
height	10cm (4in)
soil	Sandy or open-textured soils
site	Best in an open sunny spot, such as front of bed/border, rock garden, raised bed, heather garden or naturalized between shrubs, in hedgerows or grass
care	Plant late summer 7cm (3in) deep
propagation	Lift, divide and replant in late spring/early summer
relatives	*C. speciosus* 'Oxonian' is one of a number of richer coloured forms. There is an effective white one, *C. speciosus* 'Albus'

practical project

PLANNING FOR YEAR ROUND INTEREST

Aim to make the patio a stage and have a place where pots and containers can be made ready in the wings then brought in succession into the limelight when they are at an interesting stage. Evergreen shrubs and topiary specimens can also be kept there to be brought out when there is a lull in the floral display.

PRACTICAL DETAILS

If possible, it is most efficient to have all the players together in one place as this allows easier planning. The position needs to have good access for wheelbarrow or sackbarrow; a reliable hard pathway and there needs to be a water supply nearby.

Design factors
■ Plenty of room for all the pots likely to be 'in the wings'.
■ Hard standing for pots and barrows.
■ An area for use as a plunge bed for pots, either on the hardstanding or adjacent to it and sunk into the ground.

■ A bunker or container to hold the plunging material, peat, coarse sand, shredded bark or whatever is used.
■ Room to carry out work such as potting up bulbs.
■ The possibility of temporary cover in periods of severe frost or snow.
■ A small cold frame is very useful for starting a lot of container plants off and could be used as a halfway house for those raised under warm glass and needing hardening off.

PLANTS AND SEASONS

Spring This is the time of bulbous activity but there are also all the primroses and early shrubs so there should be no shortage of colour. There is still time to sow seed of bedding plants and groups of annuals *in situ* between shrubs and in spots where bulbs will die down later. Geraniums stored in frost-proof conditions can now be encouraged to grow under glass ready for placing outside once the danger of frost is passed.

SPRING CONTAINERS

Grape hyacinths (*Muscari azureum* and others)
Iris reticulata hybrids – not very long in flower but very early and bright
Narcissus early-flowered kinds, avoid doubles and tall-stemmed cultivars
Pansies and violets
Polyanthus and **primroses**
Scilla sibirica
Snowdrops (*Galanthus*)
Tulipa, early doubles, Kaufmanniana hybrids, Greigii hybrids and others, especially shorter-stemmed ones. Also
T. fosteriana 'Red Emperor', mid-spring
T. 'Artist', salmon, pink and green, sturdy, late spring
T. 'White Triumphator', lily-flowered, tall, late spring

SUMMER CONTAINERS

Pelargoniums in variety – keep out of frost
Lilium, most. Choose Asiatic hybrids to bloom in early to midsummer and Orientals for midsummer to early autumn (see p.49)
See also hanging basket plants, page 64

WINTER CONTAINERS

Topiary specimens
Euonymus fortunei, cultivars
Aucuba japonica
Conifers
Ivies
Winter-flowering heathers
Winter-flowering pansies
Primroses
Polyanthus

Summer Hanging baskets and containers are overflowing with colour from petunias, lobelia, geraniums and a host of hardy and half-hardy annuals as well as lilies and then agapanthus in late summer. Empty the spring containers of bulbs and plant them out into border positions making sure that the bulbs are now at the correct depth for outdoor life even if this means burying parts of the foliage. Replant these containers with plants for autumn and winter display. Put dwarf Michaelmas daisies in larger pots and, in late summer, plant the autumn-flowering crocuses and colchicums. Foliage shrubs like variegated euonymus can be potted and watered ready for winter duty.

Autumn Outstanding bulbous plants for the autumn are *Nerine bowdenii* and *Amaryllis belladonna*. They can be grown in beds around the patio and also do well for three or four years in containers before demanding fresh homes and a thinning. Gather up shrubs for winter effect. Choose some large winter-flowering heathers for many weeks of brightness.

Winter Evergreen shrubs, conifers and topiary specimens come into their own. Variegated shrubs can be very bright – spotted laurel, *Aucuba japonica*, is very useful, healthy and as hardy as a pig's snout. Some berried shrubs can be attractive through much of the winter; of the ones small enough to grow in containers, the Gaultherias (Pernettyas) are some of the most spectacular. *G. mucronata* forms have lots of white, pink, red and wine berries on their low intricate evergreen branches.

NOVEMBER

Days get shorter and darker, but there are still some when it is a pleasure to get outside to tackle some of the jobs that queue up at the back-end of the year. Most of the leaves have fallen; they can be collected and, if possible, put through the shredder with other garden rubbish before being taken to the compost heap. Bonfires are not for fallen leaves and other things which can be reduced into the humus that is always wanted for containers and pots and for enriching border soils.

Any day now a reminder will come to store the garden furniture for the winter. Must do that and, at the same time and while the weather is wet, it is a good idea to put away the tools, pots, composts and other items used for maintaining the patio.

All is not tidying and irksome routine, though. Flowers may still be plentiful; roses can keep on coming and this is particularly so of the small, neat patio varieties. By the house, Garrya elliptica is getting on with the job of festooning itself with long, silvery grey-green catkins and the warmth of the walls and shelter of the patio are bound to encourage winter jasmine to come fully into bloom this month, its primrose-yellow blossom brightening dark green stems. Viburnum 'Dawn' and its siblings started to open their pink-flushed white posies of scented flowers before the last of the leaves were shed. Sometimes the winter-flowering cherry, Prunus subhirtella autumnalis, will daringly reveal its first flush of blossom while the branches are still decorated with leaves in autumn golds and oranges, an attractive arrangement if somewhat unusual and fleeting.

On the patio, winter pansies begin to do their weather-defying duty while various Erica carnea cultivars have started on their long season of colour.

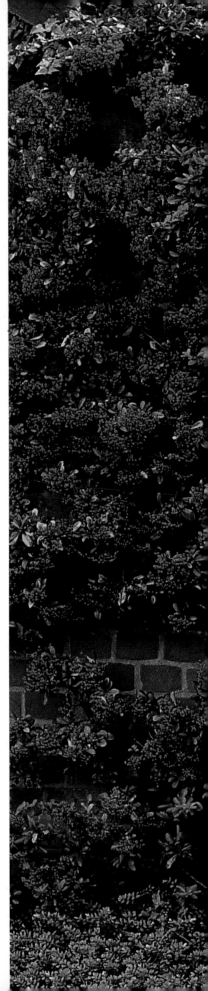

tasks
FOR THE
month

CHECKLIST

- Winter hanging baskets
- Planting shrubs and trees
- Pond care
- Coppicing shrubs and trees
- Keeping notes

WINTER HANGING BASKETS

If not already organised, you can still arrange colourful baskets for winter by planting them up with generously sized plants that will stand winter weather. Large-flowering winter pansies can provide months of bloom if the basket is positioned where dead heads can be easily removed. A number of winter-flowering heathers with golden-leaved euonymus and bushy trailing ivies will need little attention, apart from making sure that the compost does not dry out – a danger even in winter.

PLANTING SHRUBS AND TREES

While the sap is quiescent, shrubs and trees can be planted and allowed to gently settle themselves into their new stations and enable roots to get ready to invade the surrounding earthspace when temperatures warm in the spring. Although containerized plants can be planted all the year round the tradition of planting from mid-autumn until early spring, established in the days of bare-root specimens, lives on. Last month or the beginning of this can be almost ideal if the weather is good and the soil manageable.

- Excavate a hole several times larger than the container with the shrub or the dimension of the roots of a bare-rooted specimen.
- Dig over the base of the hole, taking the opportunity to incorporate humus.

- Rubble can also be dug in if it will help to keep the soil structure open.

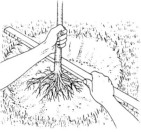

- Turn out the specimen and place it in the hole, then check that the soil level will be the same after planting as it was in the pot.

- If badly root-bound, try to ease out some of the stronger roots and direct them into the surrounds.

- With taller specimens likely to catch wind, drive in a stake for support.

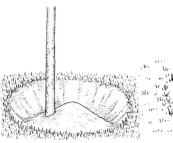

- With compost and a scattering of slow-release fertilizer, enliven the soil for returning to the hole. If your soil is amply provided with nourishment, this feed is not essential. It will certainly not be taken up quickly, the roots only become really active months ahead at the end of the winter.

- Return soil evenly around the shrub, continuing to return and firm until the original level is reached.

- Water in thoroughly and, if staked, attach it to the support with proper ties that will not restrict growth.

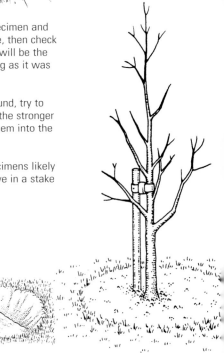

POND CARE

Dead leaves and debris need fishing out of the water. Later a floating log will make it easier to keep the surface free of overall ice, a consideration if there are fish in the pool and a help for visiting wildlife.

COPPICING SHRUBS AND TREES

There are several important garden shrubs and trees that serve better if cut down every other year or so. The dark-leaved hazel, *Corylus maxima* 'Purpurea', can be induced to grow huge leaves on strong new growth and these will be a much darker maroon-black than if nature is allowed its own course. The popular eucalypt, *E. gunnii*, if cut down, will produce a fountain of sparkling branches carrying the typical round juvenile

leaves so loved by flower arrangers. If you have space it is a good plan to have two specimens so that each can be cut down in alternate years. (See margin for list of some shrubs and trees that respond to coppicing.)

KEEPING NOTES

I have friends whose garden diaries I greatly admire. If only I was so methodical. In these diaries they list purchases — their source, price and where in the garden

they have been installed. They make notes on seed sowing. The undertaking of some piece of garden construction or reconstruction is detailed. Not only are the records of great interest to the individual, they can also teach gardening techniques and remind of plants that fail as well as the ones that succeed. I feel sure that these gardeners have learning curves that are much more healthy than mine; I never seem to have the time to make notes, but I do commend the practice.

COPPICING

- *Complete at the end of winter but the eucalypts are better done in mid-spring*
- *Cut all growth down to within about 15–20cm (6–8in)*
- *If possible have two specimens of each kind so that one can be cut back alternate years*

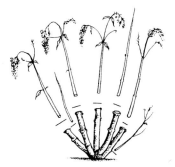

COPPICING BUDDLEIA

In early spring cut back only healthy shoots to 30cm (12in) and discard all others

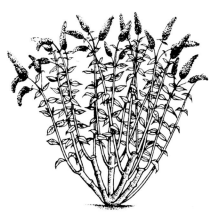

By summer the shrub will have doubled in size (above) with flowers born at the end of the new shoots

In late winter cut all shoots back to 30cm (12in) as before

SHRUBS AND TREES THAT ARE GOOD TO COPPICE

Tree of heaven (*Ailanthus altissima*) – large dark green leaves of up to 30 paired leaflets
Buddleia davidii – long, arching stems with fragrant flowers borne on long racemes
***Cornus alba* 'Elegantissima'** – red-stemmed dogwood with variegated foliage
***C. alba* 'Sibirica'** – bright red stems
***C. stolonifera* 'Flaviramea'** – olive-yellow stems
***Corylus avellana* 'Purpurea'** – very dark foliage
***C. maxima* 'Purpurea'** – very dark maroon, nearly black leaves up to 20cm (8in) long
Eucalyptus – most kinds but especially
E. cordata, wide heart-shaped or rounded silver discs, skewered onto stems
E. gunnii, juvenile circular silver coinage, adult leaves long spears
E. pulverulenta, silver-white, very broad, rounded leaves skewered onto branches often reaching out horizontally
Paulownia tomentosa – normal 30cm (12in) leaves may be replaced by some up to 1m (3ft). Best cut back at the end of winter
Sumachs (*Rhus*) such as:
Rhus glabra – large pinnate leaves of 15–29 leaflets
***R. glabra* 'Laciniata'** – with large leaves of many finely cut leaflets
R. typhina – similar pinnate leaves, brilliant autumn colours
***R. typhina* 'Laciniata'** – very finely cut leaves
***Rubus thibetanus* 'Silver Fern'**, white stems
***Salix alba* 'Britzensis'** – orange-red stems
S. alba vitellina – yellow stems
S. daphnoides – purple stems
***Sambucus nigra* 'Aurea'** – golden-leaved elder
***S. nigra* 'Guincho Purple'**, dark-leaved form

plants
OF THE
month
1

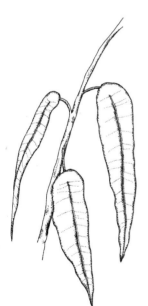

SNOW GUM
(Eucalyptus pauciflora subsp. *niphophila)*

Of all the 600-odd different species of eucalypts this must be the hardiest. It grows in Britain as if it were in Australia and there are climatic differences! It is a graceful tree and although with time it can be large, it will permit pruning.

type	Evergreen tree
flowers	Small, cream powder puffs; usually early summer
foliage	Tough, flat, pointed oval in steely greens, new young foliage is tinged orange, young stems are orange-brown
height	10m (30ft) – if allowed but can easily be kept in check
spread	3–4m (10–12ft) but can be kept pruned back
soil	Not fussy
site	Where its patchwork trunk colourings can be enjoyed and its size is not a nuisance
care	Can be cut down to encourage multiple trunks. Prune if necessary
propagation	Seed sown late winter can result in specimens over 90cm (36in) high by autumn
relatives	*E. gunnii* is popular, with rounded juvenile foliage much loved by flower arrangers. Coppice every two or three years to ensure a supply of juvenile leaves. *E. nicholii* is a very dainty tree with red young stems and very narrow long pendent leaves – the Australian answer to silver birch, but perhaps more dainty, and evergreen!

SWEET BOX
(Sarcococca confusa)

The tiny flowers of this neat winter-flowering shrub are too small to be visually dynamic but they have a lovely fragrance, so make sure you position any specimens near enough to the house to approach in winter, to enjoy the scent and to cut pieces for taking indoors.

type	Evergreen shrub
flowers/fruit	Insignificant, small, creamy white held tightly to stems, but very fragrant; midwinter followed by black berries
foliage	Highly-polished, tough, oval but pointed and dark green. Healthy and tidy

height	1m (3ft)
spread	1m (3ft)
soil	Fertile soil which keeps moist
site	In sun or shade, with heathers, shrubs, or in a bed/border
care	Carefree
relatives	*S. hookeriana* is a stronger more upright shrub, 1.5 x 2m (5 x 6ft); *S. humilis* is 1m (3ft) high and wide suckering with narrow pointed leaves and lots of tiny, white tassel flowers, heavily scented

WINTER-FLOWERING HEATHER
(Erica × darleyensis 'Silberschmelze')

Winter-flowering heathers are very good value, they last so long in good order just when we need some colour. This one makes a fine contrast of dark green and vivid white.

type	Dwarf, evergreen shrub
flowers	Crowded, brilliant white flowers in long narrow spikes; from late autumn till mid-spring,
foliage	Very dark green, ideal contrast to flowers
height	45cm (18in),
spread	At least twice as broad as its height
soil	Not fussy, will tolerate lime
site	Non-shaded: a heather bed, with shrubs, or at the edge of a bed/border

care When established can be given light trim after flowering before new growth gets underway

propagation Easiest by layering pieces, surround chosen twigs with mix of grit and peat

relatives 'Ghost Hills' is another × *darleyensis* hybrid with deep pink flowers and at least as long in bloom as 'Silberschmelze'. All *E. carnea* cultivars should also be considered for winter flowers; they are also lime-tolerant

BIRD CLAW IVY
(Hedera helix 'Sagittifolia Variegata'*)*

There are hundreds of attractive ivies to choose from. We really do not exploit them enough. Some kinds have large, heavy leaves, not so this one!

type Self-clinging, evergreen climber

flowers None

foliage Small, three-lobed, bird's foot-shaped, grey-green, edges irregularly margined with pale cream. Dense growth

height As long as a very long bit of string! Covers a wall

soil Not fussy

site Walls, tree trunks, poles, containers

care Cut back to keep within chosen limits

propagation Will layer itself at ground level. Otherwise very easy as cuttings

relatives *H. helix* 'Sagittifolia', despite its name, is not the form from which the variegated kind mutated. The plant now grown as 'Sagittifolia' is a much-branched, vigorous type with small claw-shaped leaves. Popular for pots

practical project 1

PLANNING AND PLANTING EVERGREENS

CONIFERS FOR COLOUR AND FORM

UPRIGHT

Chamaecyparis lawsoniana
'Allumii' forms
C. lawsoniana 'Erecta Viridis',
C. lawsoniana 'Green Pillar'
Juniperus communis 'Hibernica'
(Irish juniper)
J. scopulorum 'Skyrocket'
Taxus baccata (yew) **'Fastigiata'**
T. baccata 'Fastigiata Aurea', rich
green and gold
T. baccata 'Fastigiata
Aureomarginata', dark green with
a golden gleam

WEEPING

Cedrus deodora
C. deodora 'Pendula'
C. nootkatensis 'Pendula'
Taxus baccata 'Dovastoniana
Aurea', dark green with golden cast

It is an oft repeated plea of mine for gardeners to plan for the winter – knowing the other seasons will almost look after themselves. When the leaves of deciduous shrubs and trees are gone, the evergreens hold the stage. They are the most important bastions against winter's onslaught and it is difficult to over-emphasize their importance.

Evergreens are needed against the house. Some can be close to the patio and others by the pergola. The view from living rooms and the patio should show a garden with a series of colourful and interesting plants all year round. Even incarcerated indoors by cold and wet, our eyes should be able to wander from one sentinel plant to another.

COLOURS AND FORMS

The thousand and one greens are highlighted by shrubs that are heavily variegated golden or silver. Conifers are only part of the queue of evergreens applying for work. Close to the patio include glistening-leaved camellias, dark *Garrya elliptica* festooned with catkins, *Magnolia grandiflora* with large tough laurel-like foliage; lower down make a patchwork of heathers in greens, lemons, golds and flushed orange-reds. To pergola uprights and walls, tie coloured ivies, many taking on interesting pink-mauve tints in winter, and the evergreen winter-flowering *Clematis armandii*.

Conifers are available in many colours from lively gold, such as the *Chamaecyparis lawsoniana* 'Lane' to red-brown; Thujas only need the first touch of frost to change their green dresses for rusty brown and these may turn to purple before spring brings fresh greens again.

Forms are so varied. Have fun arranging a tableau with prostrate junipers and heathers, bushy camellias, pieris, rhododendrons, tree heathers, and tall upright conifers or dramatically draped weeping forms. Even the miniature landscapes in trough gardens can house tiny conifers in all sorts of forms.

CHOICE

Screens To block out or distract from displeasing views try a group of variously-coloured *Chamaecyparis lawsoniana* cultivars. Hollies can also be used, many forms growing quickly once they have had 12–18 months to get properly established. They also provide excellent wind breaks. Lower

screens can be formed by rhododendrons and camellias on acid soils. The very useful *Eleagnus pungens* 'Maculata' is reliable and brightens every winter scene with its ninety per cent golden-variegated foliage. It can be used with the dark green *Viburnum tinus* to make a dense wind shield, the viburnum having countless tight posies of scented white flowers from pink buds.

Against house walls *Magnolia grandiflora* looks splendid and goes just as high as you require. *M. grandiflora* 'Exmouth' is popular, coming into bloom as a very young specimen and remaining free flowering. With humus-enriched soils camellias enjoy the warmth and shelter of walls and will provide blossom in winter and spring especially if the flowers are sheltered from early sunshine which causes damage when combined with frost. (See also Wall Planting p.140)

Border shrubs Close to the patio some evergreens are needed to maintain a healthy balance of interest around the year.

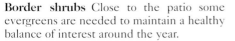

PLANTING

Planting of all trees and shrubs should be undertaken as an important rite and time taken. These plants will be around for decades, a few minutes spent now is a token to pay for future pleasure (Tasks for the Month p.124 explains how it's done).

CARE AND MAINTENANCE

Normally minimal:
- Keep weeds down, especially around newly-planted specimens.
- Mulch to conserve moisture, smother weeds and provide food.
- Prune away broken or misplaced pieces.
- Prune to encourage good form, especially providing good cover close to the ground.

CONIFERS FOR COLOUR AND FORM (continued)

PROSTRATE

Juniperus - many forms including
J. × media 'Pfitzeriana', low, thick, grey-green
J. × media 'Pfitzeriana Aurea', golden
J. × media 'Pfitzeriana Glauca', blue-green
J. squamata 'Blue Carpet', blue-green
J. virginiana 'Silver Spreader', silver-blue

BLUE-GREEN

Chamaecyparis lawsoniana 'Pembury Blue', neat, tall pyramid
Juniperus chinensis 'Blue Alps'
J. horizontalis 'Blue Chip', widespread, low, ground cover
J. squamata 'Blue Carpet', prostrate

YELLOW

Chamaecyparis lawsoniana 'Lane', neat, pyramid
C. pisifera 'Filifera Aurea', rather shaggy spreading shape
Thuja occidentalis 'Rheingold', rusty-coloured in winter, slow growing, rounded pyramid

PURPLE

Thuja orientalis 'Purple King'

plants
OF THE
month
2

**EVERGREENS FOR
BORDERS AROUND THE
PATIO**

**Strawberry tree *(Arbutus unedo,
A.* × *andrachnoides)*,** dark green
***Arundinaria nitida*, bamboo**
Spotted laurel *(Aucuba japonica)*,
polished green and yellow
***Berberis* × *stenophylla*,** small dark
leaves, orange spring blossom
Ceanothus, in variety against
walls, small dark shiny leaves,
blue blossom
Cotoneaster franchetii and others
with orange fruit
***Eleagnus pungens* 'Maculata',**
heavily gold variegated
Heathers *(Erica)*, in variety
***Erica arborea alpina*,** 1m (3ft) high
Escallonias, in variety
Hollies *(Ilex)***
***Mahonia japonica*,** handsome
pinnate leaves with spines
***M.* 'Charity',** lemon winter flowers
***M.* 'Lionel Fortesque',** winter
flowers
Pieris, especially on acid soils
Rhododendrons, especially on
acid soils

130

FATSIA
(Fatsia japonica)

This has been a favourite house plant for over
a hundred years but, being hardy, can be a very
successful garden shrub with magnificent
foliage and flowers at this time of year.

type	Evergreen shrub
flowers	Like those of ivy to which it is related, but much much larger. Milk-white, rounded heads of small flowers which can be followed by black fruit
foliage	Large, shining, rich green, divided into pointed 'fingers'. Persistent and handsome
height	3m (10ft)
spread	3m (10ft)
soil	Best in healthy well-drained soil
site	Sun or shade, but best out of strong winds. Useful in awkward corner spots
care	Easy, but best with some shelter especially in cold areas
propagation	By ground- or air layers

GARRYA
(Garrya elliptica)

This evergreen shrub is usually planted
against a wall and certainly in its first few years

it may need support but it can be grown in the
open and by this time of the year will be well
advanced with its catkins.

type	Evergreen shrub
flowers	Many very long catkins of silvery-grey and green from late autumn through the winter
foliage	Dark matt-green, oval, perhaps best against a brighter kind such as golden privet or *Aucuba japonica*
height	4m (12ft)
spread	3–4m (9–12ft)
soil	Fertile, well-drained
site	By a wall or in the open in sun or semi-shade
care	Needs support while growing a backbone but then will only need odd sprigs pruning
propagation	By layers
relatives	*G. elliptica* 'James Roof' is an especially good, long-catkined form

SKIMMIA
(Skimmia japonica)

An evergreen that has very persistent berries
and so is decorative most of the year.
Specimens are either male or female; you
need one male for up to four berrying females.

type	Evergreen shrub

flowers	Tight posies of small, pink-budded white flowers
foliage	Tough, dark green, oval
soil	Neutral or acid
site	Sun or shade
care	If foliage becomes yellow this means the shrub is being affected by free lime in the soil. Treat soil with sequestrene and top dress with compost and humus
propagation	By layers or summer cuttings
relatives	*S. japonica* 'Veitchii' (*formanii*) is a female upright, densely foliaged shrub. *S. japonica* 'Rubella' is a pollen-bearing male. *S. japonica* subsp. *reevesiana* breaks rank and has both male and female parts, its berries are attractive but less glossy

LAURUSTINUS

(Viburnum tinus)

The viburnum genus is full of good reliable shrubs, both evergreen and deciduous. This species is a trustworthy, yeoman type that can be pressed to all kinds of service, so don't be put off by its widespread use. With its extraordinary thick foliage cover, it is ideal for shelter belts or hedges and its long season of bloom through the winter makes it indispensable.

type	Evergreen shrub
foliage	Thickly furnished with smooth, oval dark green leaves
flowers	Large numbers of flat heads of pretty, small white flowers from the beginning of winter through into spring, but most prolific in the second half of winter. Pink in bud, scented
height	3m (10ft)
spread	3m (10ft)
site	Best in sun, but will tolerate some shade. Can be planted almost anywhere and is often used as a hedge or screening plant
care	Trouble-free shrub. A great favourite in Victorian times and still worth growing
propagation	Low pieces can be layered and rooted quickly – it will probably layer itself without any help – and rooted pieces can be moved to their new quarters in early spring
cultivars	There are a number of named forms. 'Gwenllian' and 'Eve Price' are the present leaders

Skimmia japonica 'Fructo Alba' *has white berries*

practical project 2

MAKING A START WITH TOPIARY

Traditionally topiary means the artificial trimming of shrubs and trees into bold geometrical shapes. Straight-groomed hedges represent the simplest form; fancy shapes, such as birds and animals, must have suggested themselves early on. Taming nature in this way has been popular for a long time. The Romans were dab hands at it and since then the idea has never died out. It was very much in vogue during Victorian times and is becoming popular again. Smaller gardens with a need to restrain the growth of some shrubs may be one reason; small gardens with buildings close by suggest formality and can be excellent for displaying topiary. Increased leisure time allows us to deal with the demands of topiary and power tools make the whole operation much easier to manage.

ROLE OF TOPIARY

It is a matter of taste whether topiary is a dominant feature around the patio or just a useful focal point. However, the patio is an ideal place for some topiary. Close to buildings topiary looks particularly impressive and living colour in strongly drawn shapes is a perfect counterpoint for the patio structure. Individual pieces can be made to act like living sculpture. The mobility of containerized topiary lends it greater utility.

SCALE AND TIMING

Box topiary, either as edging or in pots, can be small: hedges starting as low as 10cm (4in). Formidable yew examples can be as much as 3–5m (10–15ft) high and while they may look as old as the hills, they can be formed in relatively few years. Of course, such large specimens are best at a distance from the smaller patio.

Apart from buying ready-made specimens, the quickest way to create topiary is by covering a moss- or foam-covered wire form with ivy. Within a few months it will form a reasonable display, perhaps in a dome shape 45cm (18in) high.

SHRUBS FOR SHAPING

The best shrubs to use are very hardy ones with small leaves and the ability to grow back from pruning.

Top favourites are box, yew and *Lonicera*

nitida. Larger-leaved shrubs such as bay and holly are sometimes used but need more care.

Box (*Buxus sempervirens* 'Suffruticosa') has many advantages: it is compact in growth with small leaves; it is hardy and takes to the discipline of the shears well; it has steady rather than rampant growth.

Yew *(Taxus baccata)*, small leaved and richly coloured, can be excellent. It responds well to being cut and is indestructible. Even old gaunt specimens can be cut down and reformed. Leaves and berries are poisonous.

Lonicera nitida has the smallest leaves. It is a good rich colour and can be quickly formed into almost any shape. It is better for smaller topiary work. Growth is so quick and propagation from cuttings so easy that it can be used freely and may even be used as a dummy while slower-growing yew or box are maturing. It needs far more frequent clipping than the other recommended kinds.

Lonicera nitida 'Baggesen's Gold'

Holly *(Ilex aquifolium)* is very hardy with a rich polished colour and can make excellent bold geometric forms. Pick one of the smaller-leaved cultivars. It is slower growing and increasing than many shrubs and consequently may be more expensive initially. Secateurs can be used following a rough shaping with shears, the aim being to reduce the number of leaves cut to awkward fractions.

MAINTENANCE

- Keep free of pests and diseases
- Keep watered and fed with general fertilizer
- Keep free of weeds
- Trim quick-growing specimens as frequently as possible – perhaps once a month in the growing season
- Trim slow-growing plants at least twice a year

MAKING A CONE SHAPE

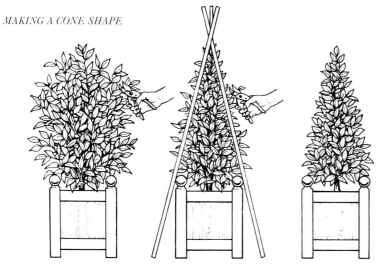

In the first year trim the plant to shape by eye. The following year make guides with canes and wire to ensure a good shape and trim again. Subsequently trim as necessary

Bay *(Laurus nobilis)* can make good cones and pyramids which look best if half-cut leaves are removed.

MAKING A ROUND SHAPE

Remove side shoots down the stem as they appear. Once the plant is the desired height remove the growing tip and shape as required

METHODS

Simple shapes may be attempted without frames, but it is usually safer to create a simple framework before beginning to cut. A cone consisting of a specimen cut into a tapered column may be achieved by eye alone. To create a simple potted cone in box:

■ Select a suitable specimen and prune away twigs that are obviously growing outside the envisaged shape.

■ Allow it to grow somewhat, perhaps for a year, then tie three or four canes to make a wigwam form over the plant. Arrange the canes close to the plant and evenly around it. They help to make sure the trimming is done evenly.

■ With hand shears or secateurs, prune away twigs outside the canes to leave the desired form. Remove the canes.

■ Repeat once or twice a year to maintain a clean outline. The specimen can be allowed to grow evenly to the size you want and is then kept in check by regular trimming.

Larger florists, wholesale florist sundries suppliers and garden centres often stock a series of wired shapes for use for topiary forms. These are fixed to hedge tops or specimen plants and the plant allowed to grow through. As growth becomes too abundant it is cut back. More fancy shapes can be made by tying in suitable branches to form envisaged shape.

SHRUBS FOR TOPIARY

Berberis thunbergii atropurpurea, especially smaller-leaved forms. Stronger ones can be used for making hedges

BOX, including
Buxus sempervirens
B. sempervirens
'Argenteovariegata', yellow-edged leaves
***B. sempervirens* 'Marginata'**, silver-edged leaves
***B. sempervirens* 'Suffruticosa'**, small leaves

IVIES, including
***Hedera helix* 'Adam'**, small leaves, well-edged silver
***H. helix* 'Buttercup'**, gold leaves
***H. helix* 'Eva',** small green and cream leaves, forward pointing, sharp lobes
***H. helix* 'Glacier'**, small leaves of silver grey, red stems
***H. helix* 'Green Feather'**, small leaves, long, pointed, centre lobe
***H. helix* 'Ivalace'**, well indented leaves, five lobes, feathery
***H. helix* 'Shamrock'**, dark green, rounded lobes

HOLLY, *Ilex aquifolium*, smaller-leaved forms and cultivars such as
***Ilex aquifolium* 'Argentea Marginata'**, white-edged leaves
***Ilex aquifolium* 'Crispa'**, leaves rather twisted
***Ilex aquifolium* 'Ovata Aurea'**, dark green and gold leaves

MORE SHRUBS FOR TOPIARY

Bay *(Laurus nobilis)*, slowish growing
Bay, golden (*L. nobilis* 'Aurea'), golden-flushed
Golden privet (*Ligustrum ovalifolium* **'Aurea')**, quick growing
Lonicera nitida, small-leaved, fast growing
***L. nitida* 'Baggesen's Gold'**, yellow-leaved , almost as fast
Yew *(Taxus baccata)*
Yew, golden (*T. baccata* 'Aurea'), golden flush from light variegation

DECEMBER

Through the kitchen window, on the patio and beyond, the world looks cold. Not snow but frost decorates all with white rime; Bathsheba considers the cat door and decides to stay in. The sempervivums, once all red and fat succulence, are now transformed, their edges marked with frozen white serrations. It makes a beautiful picture, then all melts before the mounting sun.

The patio looks well even in this cold. The stone, brick, wood and pebbles provide the structural element, birds feeding at their table capture the eye, along with potted conifers, trimmed box and cascading ivy. The design is more decorative today with the frost: the snow can wait. The patio plays an important role in its place between the house and the winter garden: from indoors it tempts us out towards the garden, from the garden it leads us to the comfort of the house.

The forms of shrubs and trees are visible in the far reaches of the garden; silver birches glow, silver-grey eucalypts glitter as their leaves move gently in the breeze. Berried shrubs sparkle in the pale winter light with warm oranges, reds and shining golds. Pyracanthas, cotoneasters, hollies, pernettyas, spindle-berries and buckthorns all have their charms. They look good even if the birds take a tithe.

Borders nearby have some of the remains of herbaceous growth: clumps of ornamental grass still look attractive though now in tones of buff and Naples yellow, Sedum spectabile is richly impressive, and even the now worn seedheads of love-in-the-mist are decorative. In the corner, Iris foetidissima bears heavy heads of gleaming scarlet beads – surely they cannot be seeds, so polished and plastic!

Close at hand, the japonica bursts into bloom, along with the so reliable Algerian iris, I. unguicularis – wretched name but such velvety smooth and charming flowers. There may be a dozen or more different plants in flower. Winter is not without its treasure.

tasks
FOR THE
month

*KEEPING PONDS ICE-FREE
Save fish and help other wildlife by keeping at least part of the pond surface free of ice with a log floating on the water's surface.*

CHECKLIST

☐ Drains
☐ Removing unwanted moss and algae
☐ Pruning shrubs
☐ Encouraging birds

DRAINS

The winter tests drainage systems, both those from the house and patio and overall drainage of flower beds. Mid-autumn's leafmould making should have ensured that you have checked all the guttering for fallen leaves and debris, if not, do this now and make sure the fall pipes and drainage grills are clear as well. If the patio paving was correctly laid it will have a slight angle to take surface water away from the house immediately and there should be sufficient hardcore drainage below to prevent any water standing around. If for any reason patio or paths have water standing after rain then mark these areas and consider making a drainage channel to take water away: introducing localized hardcore is not likely to give sufficient drainage potential; it is more likely to act as a sump.

REMOVING UNWANTED MOSS AND ALGAE

More or less permanent moisture will encourage the growth of moss and algae. While moss can look quite pleasant growing in the intersections of pavings, if it then appears on the surfaces it is likely to add to the slippery effect of the algae, making the whole treacherous underfoot. The causes of moss and algae are constant moisture and a lack of drying potential; airless sheltered places are likely to be worst affected. Cure or minimize the problem by treating the causes such as inadequate drainage or an overdone clutter of pots and containers.

Strong detergents can be purchased to clear algae. Scrub these over the surface with a strong yard brush. One or two applications will normally clear all. Do not think in terms of killing the growth with chemicals such as *Sodium chlorate*, not only does this chemical seep into surrounding ground and kill or damage plant life, but it appears to leave the treated area in a receptive state for a fresh invasion of moss and algae.

PRUNING SHRUBS

Winter allows time to prune shrubs and trees around the patio and in the garden proper. It is worth keeping a note in your garden diary to remind you which ones need attention — those with misplaced branches or ones that can be removed to improve the overall form of the shrub or increase the view of the garden and around. Other items to note are branches that grow across the centres of shrubs or trees: these need removing. Damaged pieces should be cut away. Specimens that are to be coppiced can be tackled now

if they are not in the middle of making a big contribution near the patio. The latest to tackle will be *Eucalyptus gunnii* which is best left until early or mid-spring (see p.125).

You may follow the latest advice about pruning rose beds. This is to use a power hedge trimmer to take off about half the top growth and leave all the twiggy bits that the books have been telling us to cut out for the past century or so. It has been proven that these smaller twigs, while not themselves bearers of flowers, produce healthy foliage and thus improve the metabolism of the bushes and increase their flowering potential. One is led to suspect that the same applies to other types of flowering shrubs, but it is going to take a brave gardener to adopt the practice for all; we have conditioned ourselves to enjoy the form of a shrub pruned by the dictates of received wisdom.

ENCOURAGING BIRDS

Most gardeners enjoy sharing their patch with birds and they can be encouraged with a little winter sustenance. If feeding is started it should be done regularly. Remember that birds fall into two loose categories: those that feed on the ground and those that prefer to forage above; so provide food on bird tables or other surfaces above ground and on the ground. Two or three stations will work more efficiently than one. When siting them remember that many birds like to have bushes or trees nearby as escape routes.

■ Keep one or two areas of water free of ice.

■ Hang half coconuts as bells for tits and others. (Do not

use desiccated coconut for birds as this can swell up inside them.)

- Hang out birdcakes (recipe opposite).
- Place apples, pears and similar fruit on the ground for thrushes and blackbirds.

- Put seeds loose and in fat on the bird table for feeders such as robins.

- Use hanging metal feeders of unsalted nuts for tits and others. (Plastic ones will be rapidly sabotaged by squirrels.)

- Bird seed mixtures are sold by pet shops.

- Once you start feeding continue until spring.

BIRDCAKE RECIPE

It is better to make two or three smaller cakes rather than one large one as the cake's own weight can make it come off the string. The bird cake can be placed on the bird table but this may mean the tits not getting their share.

The basic ingredients are melted suet or lard and mixed seeds. Quantities could be: approx. 250gm (8oz) suet or lard to 500gm (1lb) nuts, seeds, dried fruit, cake crumbs, oats

Method

- Use a small pudding bowl, plastic carton or a half coconut shell as a mould.

- Put a length of string long enough to reach from the bottom of the mix to the outside of the mould.

- Melt suet/lard and mix in the dry ingredients.

- Allow to cool and solidify.

- Turn out of the mould and hang from a shrub branch or bird table, using the string to ensure it is secure.

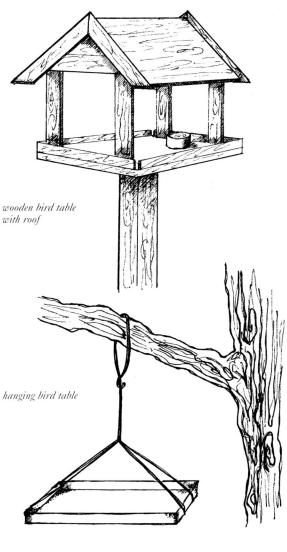

wooden bird table with roof

hanging bird table

hanging nut feeders

SUITABLE FOOD FOR THE BIRD TABLE

Beef suet
Bacon rinds (short pieces)
Tinned pet food
Mealworms
Maggots
Ants' eggs
Cheese
Hard-boiled egg
Fruit (fresh, dried or decaying)
Berries of all sorts
Peanuts (not salted): see note on
  p136
Almonds
Hazel
Brazils
Mixed seeds (the proprietary
  brands sold for cage birds)
Hemp (much appreciated, but
  which must be kept dry, eg on
  a bird table with a roof)
Canary seed
Millet, maize, corn and sunflower
  seeds
Rice
Potatoes (boiled or baked in their
  skins
Stale cake crumbs
Coconut in the shell (not dessicated)
Biscuit and breadcumbs
Coarse oats (raw, not cooked)

plants
OF THE
month

MAHONIA
(Mahonia × media 'Charity'*)*

A series of hybrid mahonias bred from *M. lomariifolia* and *M. japonica*, these are stalwart winter performers and fine foliage plants at other times. 'Charity' is the best known but the others are equally as good.

type	Evergreen shrub
flowers	Plenty of upright sprays of crowded lemon-scented, cup-shaped, lemon-yellow flowers at the branch ends; autumn through winter. Sprays tend to widen out more horizontally as the flowers open
foliage	Handsome flat leaves of perhaps 17–19 flat, sharply-toothed leaflets, rich green, tough
height	3m (10ft)
spread	1–2m (3–6ft)
soil	Not fussy
site	Sun or shade, with other shrubs or as a specimen
care	If single-stemmed and looking like a miniature palm tree, it can be cut back to 18cm (6in) or thereabouts to encourage several new erect stems
propagation	Air layering or eye-cuttings (a leaf with bud close to stem) treated as normal cuttings
relatives	Several very good siblings: *M. × media* 'Buckland' is another strong one with long seasons of bloom; *M. × media* 'Lionel Fortesque' has long sprays, usually held slightly more erectly

UNIVERSAL PANSY
(Viola × wittrockiana)

These charming pansies will bloom through winter and are especially good in milder spells, or in containers in sheltered spots. For the best results, plant early or get well established plants, small specimens planted late will rarely have enough 'get up and go'.

type	Hardy annuals
flowers	Wide range of plain coloured or

bicolours, with darker centres

foliage	Dark green, typical pansy leaves
height	15–22cm (6–9in)
spread	15–30cm (6–12in)
soil	Use good compost with slow-release fertilizer
site	Beds/borders, raised beds, containers or hanging baskets
care	Sow seed in summer to have plants for flowering in winter. They can also be used for summer bedding if sown in autumn or late winter
relatives	V. × wittrockiana 'Floral Dance' is a hardy strain, recently improved, and is neat and free of bloom

EUONYMUS

(Euonymus fortunei 'Emerald 'n' Gold'*)*

This is a very adaptable shrub that looks especially bright in the winter months. It can be grown in containers, even in hanging baskets, and makes dense ground cover or can be pruned into a low hedge or persuaded to grow up the wall to the bedroom windows.

type	Variegated, evergreen spreading shrub
flowers	Insignificant
foliage	Oval leaves predominantly rich gold but with bright green centres. In winter the leaves take on a blushing pinky mauve hint
height	60cm (24in); 3m (10ft) or more up a wall with some support
spread	Double the height or more
soil	Not fussy
site	Best colour in an open position. Good near house walls or in beds/borders or close by the patio
care	Trim to keep within required limits
propagation	Easy from layers, also from summer cuttings
relatives	There is a range of good E. fortunei cultivars: 'Emerald Gaiety' is bushy, making a very thick mass of foliage 1m (3ft) high and twice as wide. The dark green central part of the leaf is widely banded with pale cream or white

CYDONIA/ JAPONICA

(Chaenomeles 'Knap Hill Scarlet'*)*

The quinces are a very useful set of shrubs; although basically early spring-flowering if planted against a wall or some such warm site,

they will usually start opening buds in the late autumn and certainly in early winter. The walls help to ripen wood and encourage the production of a mass of flower buds.

type	Deciduous shrub
flowers/fruit	Vivid deep red bowl-shaped flowers with central boss of golden stamens. On a wall from late autumn until early spring. Some produce hard fat quinces, green turning olive yellow
foliage	Oval, shiny, dark green
height	1.5m (5ft)
spread	3m (10ft)
soil	Not fussy
site	Sun and well-drained site
care	Wall specimens: cut back shoots after flowering to two buds and keep shortening new growth through the growing year to keep the shrub tidy against the wall
propagation	Easiest to layer a low branch, grazing a portion and treating this with rooting powder
relatives	Plenty of good cultivars: C. speciosa 'Nivalis', pure white; C. speciosa 'Simonii', dense dwarf form with blood-red blossom; C. speciosa 'Apple Blossom', white and pink

practical project

WALL PLANTING

SHRUBS ENJOYING WALL SUPPORT

Actinidia kolomikta
Ceanothus dentatus
C. rigidus
Japonica/Quince *(Chaenomeles)*
Escallonia macranthus
Euonymus fortunei
Jasmine
Pyracantha
Roses, rambling and climbing

SELF-CLINGING SHRUBS, WITH AERIAL ROOTS UNLESS STATED
Asteranthera ovata
Campsis, the following are better with ties:
C. grandiflora; C. 'Flamingo'
C. 'Madame Galen'; C. radicans
Decumaria barbara, evergreen
D. sinensis, evergreen
Ercilla volubilis
Euonymus radicans
Hedera canariensis; H. colchica
H. helix, many kinds
Hydrangea anomala petiolaris
H. serratifolia
Parthenocissus henryana, tendrils with sucker pads
P. quinquefolia, tendrils with sucker pads
Pileostegia viburnoides
Schizophragma hydrangeoides
S. integrifolium

The wall is a new garden. Even without any soil below, it can be hung with baskets and be home for large cradles full of a wide variety of plants. On a paved base, half barrels can hold shrubs that will lean against the wall or climb up it. With a little soil beside them, the walls greatly increase the numbers of climbers, shrubs, herbaceous and bulbous plants we can grow.

In a width of just 45–60cm (18–24in) and a more or less similar depth of healthy soil, almost anything can be grown. Many interesting and beautiful shrubs that just about manage in the open garden will flourish near the wall where their wood is ripened more easily and they are kept comfortably warm. Here, they reveal themselves as extrovert bloomers despite being terribly inhibited and shy in the open. The warmth, shelter and wood ripening propensities of wall-side sites are to the good, but there are the possible disadvantages of dry conditions and poor soil if this has not been extensively enriched.

Different walls will enjoy different characteristics; those near the patio can be assumed to be warm and sunny. Think of the wall in three parts: the base where wall planting is done and where herbaceous plants have a look in between stems of shrubs; the lower part of the wall where free-standing shrubs such as camellias may hold sway; the upper reaches where, with their own clinging tendrils or with the aid and support of trellis or wires, taller shrubs and climbers reach to upper windows and the gutters – wisterias twine and Virginia creepers creep.

PLANT SUPPORTS

Although there are plenty of plants that can cope by themselves against a wall, ramblers, scramblers, climbers and wobbly shrubs must have support. This support must be reliable and safe. If possible it should be almost invisible and certainly not intrusive; failing this it should be neat and pleasing to the eye. It should be designed to need as little maintenance as possible.

There are two main methods of support: a series of taut wires held close to the wall or a form of trellis work through which plants can grow or to which they can be attached. A third, less satisfactory, option may be to use masonry nails wherever they are needed. Some are made with easily bent leaden tops which can help to hold a stem.

Lower parts
Most of the action is in the first 2–3m (6–9ft) of wall. Winter jasmine *(Jasminum nudiflorum)* can easily run up a wall with support. It is invaluable for winter colour. In spring a very pleasing picture can be created from the arching wands of *Forsythia suspensa* that without help would be scrawling around the ground with all the appearance of a broken backbone. After a few seasons building up its skeleton of branches close to the wall, the shrub produces early spring yellow blossom on falling shoots.

Tall walls
Roses might be a first choice. In bloom they can be wonderful. Ceanothus and pyracantha cultivars will go high up walls and can give a denser cover.

PLANTING

Climbers and ramblers are best planted with their roots away from the base, perhaps 30cm (12in), with the roots widely spread pointing away from the wall and the stem led to the wall.

In healthy soil, shrubs should get away easily if given an initial thorough watering and subsequently not allowed to dry out. Roots will explore the soil and then deeper ones will reach out under paving or other surface barriers.

MAINTENANCE

- Keep weed free.
- Maintain a compost mulch.
- Give a light annual sprinkle of general fertilizer.
- After flowering, prune back flowering stems of winter jasmine, *Forsythia suspensa*, *Chaenomeles* and other winter to early spring bloomers to two basal buds.
- Wisteria needs leafy whippy summer growth severely cut back in late summer, leaving only the stems needed to extend the plant. In winter remove any stems developed since summer. Cut back and reduce summer pruned branches to one or two buds. Train horizontally.
- Roses. Cut away diseased or fractured twigs. Try to bring main growths lower, closer to the horizontal to encourage flowering and fresh upward growth.

CLIMBERS AND SHRUBS FOR COLD WALLS

Acradenia frankliniae
Asteranthera ovata
Berberidopsis corallina
Billardiera longiflora
Camellia japonica
C. sasanqua
C. × williamsii hybrids
Clematis, various
Clerodendrum thomsoniae
Cotoneaster, various including
C. horizontalis
C. × watererii
Decumaria barbara
D. sinensis
Drimys winteri
Escallonia macrantha
E. iveyi
Hedera, various
Hop (*Humulus lupulus***)**
Hydrangea anomala petiolaris
Jasminum nudiflorum
Lapageria rosea
Lonicera **(honeysuckle)**, various including:
L. × americana
L. × brownii
L. sempervirens
L. × tellmanniana
Olearia solandri
Osmanthus, various
Parthenocissus, various
Philodendron
Pileostegia viburnoides
Pyracantha (firethorn) various
Schisandra, various
Viburnum, various
Vitis coignetiae

HERBACEOUS PLANTS AND BULBS ENJOYING WALLS

For main bulbs see p37, 109
Amaryllis belladonna
Eucomis, various
Habranthus
Iris unguicularis, all forms
Lycoris squamigera
Nerine bowdenii
Scilla peruviana
Watsonia, various
Zephyranthes, various

Other South African corms and bulbs are better in the shelter of walls including small-flowered *Gladiolus* species

USEFUL ADDRESSES

We are well served in this country by garden centres and nurseries for all our plant requirements. If in any doubt consult *The Plant Finder* for suppliers of more unusual plants. This invaluable book, published annually by Royal Horticultural Society, suggests possible sources for almost every plant. There is only space here to list just a few of the many good suppliers of roses and bulbs.

ROSES

David Austin Roses Ltd, Bowling Green Lane, Albrighton, Wolverhampton, West Midlands WV7 3HB
Peter Beales Roses, London Road, Attleborough, Norfolk NR17 1AY
Fryer's Nurseries Ltd, Manchester Road, Knutsford, Cheshire WA16 0SX
Gandy's Roses, North Kilworth, Lutterworth, Leicestershire LE17 6HZ
R Harkness and Co Ltd, The Rose Gardens, Hitchin, Hertfordshire SG4 0YA

BULBS

Jacques Amand Ltd, The Nurseries, 145 Clamp Hill, Stanmore, Middlesex HA7 3JS
Avon Bulbs, Burnt House Farm, Mid Lambrook, South Petherton, Somerset TA13 5HE

Bloms Bulbs, Primrose Nursery, Park Lane, Sharnbrook, Bedfordshire MK44 1LW
Broadleigh Gardens, Bishops Hull, Taunton, Somerset TA4 1AE
De Jager, The Nursery, Marden, Kent TN12 9BP

KNOT GARDENS

The properties listed have knot gardens or gardens contained within mini-hedges that are close to the knot garden style. Many more can be found by looking through the National Trust property guides or the yellow book 'Gardens of England and Wales' published by the National Gardens Scheme Charitable Trust.

Bishop's Palace, Hatfield
Blenheim Palace, Oxfordshire
Cranbourne Manor, Dorset
Drummond Castle, near Crieff, Perthshire
Dyrham Park, Gloucestershire
Edzell Castle, Angus
Hampton Court, London
Hanbury Hall, Worcestershire
Hidcote, Gloucestershire
Levens Hall, Cumbria (famous for topiary)
Pitmedden, Aberdeenshire
Rousham Park, Steeple Aston, Oxfordshire
Tudor House Museum, Bugle Street, Southampton

INDEX

INDEX

INDEX